Both **Leonard J. Basile** and **Anne S. Cernak** are elementary school teachers and have lectured extensively on the design and creation of learning materials for elementary school students. They have conducted numerous workshops and written several articles on education.

LEONARD J. BASILE
ANNE S. CERNAK

THE TEACHER'S IDEA CATALOG

HOW TO CREATE LEARNING MATERIALS FOR YOUNG CHILDREN

PRENTICE HALL, INC., Englewood Cliffs, New Jersey 07632

Library of Congress Cataloging in Publication Data

Basile, Leonard J.
The teacher's idea catalog.

"A Spectrum book."
Bibliography: p. 159
1. Teaching—Aids and devices—Design and construction.
I. Cernak, Anne S. II. Title.
LB1043.B34 1982 372.13'078 82-12220
ISBN 0-13-888511-7
ISBN 0-13-888503-6 (pbk.)

With love, we dedicate this
book to our parents.

This book can be made available to businesses and organizations
at a special discount when ordered in large quantities.
Contact: Prentice-Hall, Inc.,
General Book Marketing, Special Sales Division,
Englewood Cliffs, New Jersey 07632

A SPECTRUM BOOK

Printed in the United States of America

10 9 8 7 6 5 4 3

ISBN 0-13-888511-7

ISBN 0-13-888503-6 {PBK.}

Cover and interior illustrations by Charles R. Lewis.
Cover design by Jeannette Jacobs. Manufacturing buyer: Cathie Lenard.

Prentice-Hall International, Inc., *London*
Prentice-Hall of Australia Pty. Limited, *Sydney*
Prentice-Hall Canada Inc., *Toronto*
Prentice-Hall of India Private Limited, *New Delhi*
Prentice-Hall of Japan, Inc., *Tokyo*
Prentice-Hall of Southeast Asia Pte. Ltd., *Singapore*
Whitehall Books Limited, *Wellington, New Zealand*
Editora Prentice-Hall do Brasile LTDA., *Rio de Janeiro*

CONTENTS

FOREWORD

Concern for the development of individual children is central to our educational system. Yet, in the practical reality of schools, an environment can exist wherein some students excel while the potential of others goes unrealized. Fortunately, Leonard Basile and Anne Cernak have written a sensitive and useful book of ideas that will help teachers to inspire *all* children to achievements that go far beyond their previous accomplishments.

This book is for educators in school and non-school settings who believe that the creative process of designing learning materials will result in an educational environment that is responsive to the unique academic and personal needs of young children. *The Teacher's Idea Catalog* assists teachers to become curriculum decision makers by designing and constructing learning materials that are tailor-made for the children they serve. The authors believe that educators who are closest to children are in the best position to decide what conditions and happenings are likely to encourage learning. Hence, this book stimulates teachers to be key decision makers in the education enterprise. Sound reasoning is given for why and how teachers can make the curriculum even more responsive by creating learning materials. Also, the authors recognize that learning takes place in settings outside the school. Several specific ways that self-made materials can be successfully implemented in the home and community are suggested. Further, the encouragement for teacher leadership in curriculum development is complemented by more than 100 detailed and workable "ideas" for improving the language and mathematics skills of young children. The ideas are clearly advanced so that teachers can select or redesign activities that are likely to lead to a stimulating educational environment.

Leonard Basile and Anne Cernak are obviously talented and resourceful teachers. We are fortunate that they shared their thoughts about promoting quality curricula. Now increasing numbers of teachers can tap this excellence that ensures the ability of schools to reach all children. This book reflects a dedication to learning and to helping others learn that made us choose education over another profession.

Robert L. Sinclair
Professor of Education and
Director of the Center for
Curriculum Studies
University of Massachusetts
Amherst, MA

PREFACE

This book is a guide, manual, and reference book of ideas rolled into one. In addition to numerous "ready-to-make" ideas, it provides a collection of techniques, methods, materials, and procedures for the creation of innovative and effective learning materials for young children.

The many reasons to create learning materials and their immediate and long-term benefits for the child are highlighted as well as hints and suggestions for using the materials within either the school or the home setting. A systematic approach for the development of useful and purposeful learning materials is featured. Through this step-by-step approach, ideas, techniques, methods, and materials are organized and presented as a guide in the design and construction of unique and exciting learning materials. This step-by-step approach includes the following six major components:

Step 1. Gather Information About the Learner
Step 2. Specify the Skill and Purpose
Step 3. Select a Theme
Step 4. Plan, Lay Out, and Construct the Material
Step 5. State the Task
Step 6. Evaluate.

In addition to the approach, an abundance of creative learning material ideas are provided and categorized into one of four types: File Folder Activities, Task Cards, Game Boards, and Manipulative Devices. Each idea presented includes its specific skill concentration, purpose and use for the learner, materials needed to make it, and a detailed description for its construction. Illustrations are provided for many of the learning materials in order to show unique ideas and to demonstrate specific techniques in design and construction. Following each idea are additional activities for the child to do based upon the skill concentration and suggestions for you about various other uses and adaptations of the material as well as suggestions for developing additional activities.

Whether you are a teacher, parent, or any one of many others involved in the education and care of children, this book provides both insight into the benefits and uses of creative learning materials and the practical knowledge needed to design and construct them.

The importance of "hands on" learning for the child is stressed and it is demonstrated how learning materials can be created to promote such a "learning by doing" environment—one that encourages the child to think, solve, create, imagine, explore, discover, and manipulate to learn.

The focus throughout the book is on developing learning materials individualized to meet the learner's specific skill needs, interest, and learning style. You will discover ways to identify and to ultimately utilize these elements within the design of the materials. By incorporating them, you will be creating highly motivational, challenging, and successful learning tools.

The step-by-step approach will guide you from beginning to end on "how to" develop, design, and construct effective learning materials. Each step is packed with valuable suggestions, tips, and techniques to consider as well as with suggested applications for their use within the design of the materials. To assure completeness and thoroughness, following each step, there appears a series of questions regarding the various elements within it.

To get you started in your creative endeavors and also to provide you with a continual source of unique and interesting ideas, an abundance of "ready-to-make" learning materials is provided. Each idea demonstrates the application of the components within the step-by-step approach along with unique techniques in design and construction. Although focused on a specific skill and purpose, each idea can readily be adjusted to meet a variety of skill needs, learning styles, and interests.

Of special significance is the organizational format throughout the book. Each concept, component, or idea is presented clearly, in sequence, and in easy to understand terms. Topics, discussions, and ideas are enhanced through numerous examples and illustrations provided to focus on the practical application and/or implementation of the various suggestions. This book combines and organizes in one volume the many techniques and methods necessary to develop creative and effective learning materials. It is not simply an idea book. "All purpose" in nature, it is intended to be utilized

- *as a guide* to provide direction and order to the many components necessary to create successful learning materials along with suggestions to effectively and practically use these for any occasion within the teaching/learning process.

- *as a manual* to equip you with the practical tools and techniques needed and "how to" use these to design and construct learning materials.
- *as a reference book of ideas* to provide you with a continual source of creative learning material ideas based on specific skills as well as numerous suggestions and methods for additional activities and skill reinforcement strategies.

ACKNOWLEDGMENTS

First and foremost, we would like to express our appreciation to our families for their understanding and patience throughout the writing of this book. Without their support and thoughtfulness, completion of this work would not have been possible.

For their guidance and influence on our work, we would like to recognize the following individuals: Gerald Bouthilette, Principal, Northampton Public Schools; Richard Albano, Director of Special Education, Northampton Public Schools; Robert Sinclair, Ed.D., Director, Center for Curriculum Studies, University of Massachusetts; and Kathleen Kirley, SSJ, Director of Continuing Education, College of Our Lady of the Elms.

Appreciation is also extended to the many children we have had the privilege to help learn during our combined twenty-five years of teaching. Each child played an important part in challenging and/or inspiring us to create new and interesting learning materials to enhance the teaching/learning process. Much of this book is the result of those efforts.

A special thanks is extended to a good friend, James R. Jensen, for his generous advice and guidance, but most especially for providing a haven for rest and relaxation.

Finally, we are grateful to Mary Kennan for her direction, guidance, and confidence in us and in our ability to "put to print" these many ideas.

I
CREATIVE
LEARNING
MATERIALS
Basic Principles
and Techniques

CREATING LEARNING MATERIALS FOR ALL OCCASIONS

Whether used to enhance a reading or mathematics curriculum or to meet an individual learner's needs, creative learning materials are valuable and exciting tools to use for all occasions.

In any instructional setting, be it traditional self-contained, an open-classroom environment, a special program, day school, or home learning, creative learning materials provide a dimension to the teaching/learning process that creates a "learning-by-doing" environment. Hence, creative learning materials are useful and applicable for individualized instruction, peer instruction, parent/child instruction, small-group instruction, and large-group instruction.

Within these instructional settings, skill attainment and development is supported and reinforced by the use of creative learning materials that, by design, will interest, motivate, and challenge learners to *think, solve, create, question,* and *experience.*

The following list suggests some of the many occasions within the teaching/learning process that prompt the creation of learning materials:

- introduction of a new skill
- reinforcement of one or several skills
- practice and/or drill of a skill
- experience in application and problem solving
- introduction of an area of study
- enhancement of points within a unit of study
- enrichment of a skill, subject area, or unit
- presentation of factual information
- review of one or several skills
- alternate method of instruction
- alternate procedure for learning

THE REASONS TO CREATE

The reasons and purposes that prompt the design and development of learning materials will vary depending on program needs and, more specifically, on learner needs. To increase your understanding and appreciation of the many possibilities, the following list and subsequent explanations highlight the important reasons to create learning materials:

- to enhance the curriculum
- to meet individual learner needs
- to create a "learning-by-doing" environment
- to motivate, challenge, and excite learners
- to provide an alternative method or approach
- to promote independent study
- to develop and strengthen skills
- to provide enrichment
- to foster creativity

TO ENHANCE THE CURRICULUM

The content or subject matter, as well as the methods of instruction and procedures for learning, make up the curriculum for a particular area of study. These components within the curriculum can be enhanced through the creation of learning materials. A math curriculum, therefore, which includes the learning of specific addition or subtraction facts, can incorporate an exciting game or activity to promote necessary drill and reinforcement. Word attack skills within a reading and language arts curriculum can be strengthened by unique and interesting projects and activities designed for skill development.

Regardless of the area of study, learning materials can be created that promote, strengthen, and/or extend the learning process. Some curriculum areas in which creative learning materials are well-suited include:

Reading and Language Arts (Spelling, Language, Phonics, Penmanship)
Mathematics

Social Studies (History, Geography)
Science
Health and Safety
Art
Music
Foreign Language

TO MEET INDIVIDUAL LEARNER NEEDS

Each child is unique in the way she or he learns. One learner may learn best when tasks and activities are concrete, and another when tasks and activities are more open-ended and abstract. One may learn visually (by seeing), and another auditorially (by hearing). In addition, rate of learning or pace and most importantly, that which interests and consequently motivates a learner, often differs considerably from one to the next.

Differences in learning style and interest can be successfully addressed within the design of carefully created learning materials. A series of task cards, for example, may be suitably developed to challenge a learner to investigate one or more historical events; or, a game board may be created to provide extra drill and practice of the multiplication tables; and, a file folder activity may be designed to promote independent study of how electricity was discovered.

TO CREATE A "LEARNING-BY-DOING" ENVIRONMENT

To learn, a child needs to explore, analyze, investigate, and manipulate. Through active participation, learning goes beyond mere *knowing* to *experiencing*. Consequently, learning should include "hands on" activities that allow the learner to touch, shape, mold, and create as part of the learning process.

By design, learning materials can establish such a "learning-by-doing" environment through which the stage is set for *action* in learning. This action may range from piecing together a math puzzle or sorting colors to creating a word mobile or storybook collage. In any event, the learner has something *to do* to learn.

TO MOTIVATE, CHALLENGE, AND EXCITE LEARNERS

To advance learning through the introduction of new skills, practice for skill development or the application of skills requires tasks and activities that will *activate* the learning process. Thus, learning methods or materials should be provided that will *motivate* a learner to do or complete a task, *challenge* a learner to try, and/or *excite* a learner to perform.

Learning materials, based on learner interest and need, can serve as the incentive or motivational "charge." The thrill of downhill skiing via a game board or the challenge of a car race on a file folder activity may be the "charge" necessary to stimulate and activate the learning process.

TO PROVIDE AN ALTERNATIVE METHOD OR APPROACH

A child, like us, needs variety in the manner in which she or he learns. Methods and approaches should change not only to fit the occasions of learning, but also to provide different and unique experiences. Through variations in approaches and methods, learner interest in the tasks, attention, and focus are increased. Thus, the often "humdrum" paper-and-pencil tasks can be replaced by learning games, projects, and activities.

TO PROMOTE INDEPENDENT STUDY

A key component within the learning process is to provide learners with the opportunity for independent study. To promote and increase self-study skills, learners should be provided with (1) motivational and interesting tasks, (2) tasks and activities in which they can be successful, and (3) time to work independently. These three elements may be different for each learner and consequently require careful planning and consideration. Through specifically designed learning materials, however, these elements and differences can be met and utilized to foster independent study. Specific tasks and/or activities can be constructed to combine a special interest with skill development. To illustrate this point, consider as an example a learner who enjoys the sport of skating. The learner is presented with a series of task cards that include word problems based on the sport. The interest in the sport captivates and challenges the learner to solve the problems.

TO DEVELOP AND STRENGTHEN SKILLS

In addition to the initial introduction of a skill or area of study, practice and application of the skill is required to assure mastery. Such mastery is developed and strengthened by providing the learner with purposeful practice activities, drill exercises, enrichment projects, and other skill reinforcement materials. By design, learning materials can be created to specifically (1) introduce a skill, (2) provide practice of a skill for mastery, or (3) enrich skill development through application.

TO PROVIDE ENRICHMENT

The scope and direction of the curriculum may be broadened and extended through enrichment activities. Such activities provide unique learning opportunities that generate new interest and foster organizational skills, analytical thinking, logical thinking, creative thinking, and imagination within the learner.

Creative learning materials can offer learners the incentive for exploration, investigation, experimentation, comprehension, and analysis through "hands on" activities and tasks designed to "point the way" for such learning. A task card or file folder activity of a current event such as a presidential election, for example, can lead to the study of the Party System, or to an investigation of the rights and responsibilities regarding voting, or even prompt the learner to conduct a mock election for analysis.

TO FOSTER CREATIVITY

Imagination and creative expression are important elements for the development of individuality. Through these elements, a child's self-identity, as well as his or her self-confidence, worth, and esteem, is strengthened.

The creativity within each child should be recognized and fostered. Creative learning opportunities, suggested and provided within learning materials, serve to *spark* the imagination and creative expression within the learner. Tasks and activities can be provided that prompt the child to pretend, imagine, respond, suggest, express, and most of all, *create*. Through interesting pictures or objects to write about, open-ended questions and thoughts to respond to, or art projects to create, the child is allowed a "free hand" to learn.

In any event, learning materials are the tools of teaching that by their design can create a world of learning for any reason.

A LOOK AT THE VALUES AND BENEFITS FOR THE CHILD

How a child learns is as important as, and perhaps more important than, what a child learns. The activity or process of learning can have a direct influence on how a child feels about learning, as well as about himself or herself and others. This influence, although oftentimes not immediately observable, can be significant, long-lasting, and affect the quality of life for the child.

The following list of values and benefits of teacher-constructed learning materials reflects both the immediate and long-lasting influences on the child.

Promotes a Positive Attitude Toward Learning. By design, tasks and activities are enjoyable and success is assured. Through pleasurable and successful learning, the child approaches tasks with confidence, is willing to try and is able to complete the task with little or no assistance. This promotes a positive attitude toward learning.

Provides Skill Development. Depending upon purpose, the child learns a new skill, receives reinforcement of a skill or skill area, or gains practice in the application of previously learned skills.

Increases Attention to Tasks. Projects, tasks, and activities are motivating, challenging, and exciting; therefore the learner's interest in a task is held, resulting in increased concentration and attention span.

Develops Organizational Skills. By design, tasks and activities are presented in order, with clarity and oftentimes with clues. Through such guided learning experiences, the learner develops skills in organization and planning.

Increases Independent Study. Motivational and stimulating tasks, based on interest, excite the learner to perform and attend through independent study. The learner is encouraged to seek out and acquire factual information and reasons for occurrences or solutions to problems.

Improves Self-Worth. Through successful performance on tasks, such as completing assignments, finding answers or solutions, comprehending, and creative expression, the child's self-appreciation and worth as a productive and contributing individual improves.

Heightens Curiosity. By design, activities and tasks challenge, excite, and stimulate curiosity within the learner. The learner is encouraged to seek out, inquire, investigate, compare, and analyze for solutions, causes, or reasons.

Promotes a Willingness to Try. Clever and interesting tasks are enjoyable to the learner and therefore prompt the learner to try or attempt new experiences. Also, due to success and achievement on tasks, the avenues of learning become inviting to the learner and promote participation.

Fosters Creativity. The child has a creative side that can and should be expressed. Through thought-provoking and stimulating open-ended or abstract-type tasks, the child's creative expression flourishes.

Encourages New Interests. Tasks and activities include or direct the learner to new and exciting areas of study. Through such exposure, the learner's general fund of knowledge is increased and enhanced.

Promotes Retention of Information. By the interesting and unique manner in which the information is presented, the learner's retention and learning capacity is extended. Also, since the learner can be presented with the same skill or skill area through a variety of tasks, retention is increased.

Fosters Socialization. By design, the child can perform the tasks and activities within a group with one or more children. Through peer involvement, the child develops such socialization skills as cooperation, sportsmanship and fair play, communication, and appropriate interaction.

Develops Independence. Through careful planning and considerations, tasks are provided that the learner may perform and complete from beginning to end with little or no help and be successful. Such tasks promote a sense of "can do" on the part of the learner. By continual success and accomplishments through self-study, the learner realizes her or his potential to act and/or perform independently.

Promotes Decision Making. Providing choices and alternatives in learning procedures as well as encouraging differences in expression or performance results promotes decision-making skills. A child needs opportunities to make choices in not only *what* is learned, but also in *how* it is learned. Specifically designed learning materials can provide suggestions and alternatives to promote sound decision making.

Develops a Sense of Security. A child needs to feel safe and secure in any environment. Within the learning environment, this fact is realized through tasks, activities, and experiences that promote and accept differences, allow assistance and cooperative learning, and that are also concrete, predictable, and success-oriented.

Develops and Strengthens Relationship with Helping Adult. Through sharing, cooperation, and acceptance, the learner realizes and values the parent, friend, teacher, or other concerned individual as friend and teacher.

USING LEARNING MATERIALS IN THE SCHOOL, HOME, AND COMMUNITY

Within any instructional setting, be it a traditional self-contained classroom, special class, open-classroom environment, learning center, therapy group, day-care center, nursery school program, or home and community learning, creative learning materials can be utilized in a variety of ways to effectively enhance the teaching/learning process. A program can be built around the continual use of learning materials or several can be provided for supplemental and reinforcement work. In any event, however, their use requires careful planning and organization to assure their effectiveness and resulting success for the learner.

The following discussion suggests several specific ways in which creative learning materials can be successfully implemented within the school, home, and community. Also presented are some hints and techniques to consider in planning and organizing the learning environment for their effective implementation.

SPECIFIC WAYS TO IMPLEMENT CREATIVE LEARNING MATERIALS IN THE SCHOOL

Use for Daily Assignments. Use creative learning materials for daily assignments such as math, spelling, and phonics tasks. These materials can provide the drill, reinforcement, and practice necessary for skill development and they are a good alternative or supplement to standard workbooks, worksheets, textbooks, or board work.

To implement, leave a note on the learner's assignment sheet, desk, or work area directing her or him to do a specific task card, file folder activity, or manipulative device. Provide skill cards and a game board for several children to use to review a specific skill, such as the addition facts. For the learner who has difficulty copying and writing, assign several different manipulative devices.

Use Within Instructional Lessons. As well as individualized instruction, creative learning materials can be used effectively in both small and large group lessons. Within these instructional settings, learning materials are useful as a motivational tool to foster interest in the lesson and increase attention to the subject. Depending upon use within the lesson, learning materials can be designed to introduce the skill area, prompt group participation, and/or be the culminating activity.

Schedule an Activity Period. Schedule a certain time block or period each day or week for all the children within the particular educational setting to use learning materials. During this time, assign special tasks and activities to each child based upon skill need.

Give a "Task a Day". Give a "task a day" to the learner who needs drill and reinforcement in a specific skill or skill area. Instead of providing different learning materials daily, section off one learning tool such as a large object task card and write several tasks on it for daily use. Have the learner complete one task or series of tasks each day.

Give a "Task a Week". Give a "task a week" to the learner for enrichment. A special project, taking from one to several days to complete, can be written on a decorative task card. Allow the learner time each day to work on the project and provide the various materials and references required. At the end of the week, the completed project can be shared with peers.

Allow Learner to "Select a Task". Arrange several learning materials, designed to meet the learner's specific needs and interest, on a table or bookshelf. Have the learner select the one he or she wants to use.

Use for "Free-Time Activity". Provide learning materials for children to use when they have completed regular assignments and have free time. A special corner of the room or project table can be set up for this purpose.

Set Up a Learning Center. A learning center is a special area set up in a classroom or educational setting where children can go and work independently on various tasks, activities, and projects designed for skill development. Both the center and the activities within it are based on a central theme of interest to the children such as sports, wild animals, dinosaurs, astronomy, or holidays. Sample titles for centers include: "Sports-Rama," "Dandy Dinosaur Center," "Star Gazer Center," and "Holiday Sparkler." The various creative activities can be multileveled (simple skills to more complex), multidisciplined (different subject areas), or can concentrate on one area of study or skill. Centers can be used for individualized instruction, assigned tasks, or as a free-time activity area.

Provide an Enrichment Box. Provide an enrichment box for learners interested in a specific topic or area of study. The enrichment box is constructed by covering a box of any size with plain paper and writing tasks on its sides. Inside the box place any materials that may be needed to complete the tasks. A large plain shopping bag can be used as a substitute for the box.

Provide Tasks for Holidays or Special Occasions. When a holiday or special occasion approaches, provide learning materials appropriate to the theme of the event. Such materials can include game boards or file folder activities that incorporate the special occasion within the design of the materials or seasonal task cards and activities.

Use for Home Tasks. Have you ever heard the comment "I didn't have time to do my homework"? Maybe the reason for this excuse is that the learner wants something other than a paper and pencil assignment. In place of assigned written homework, let the learner take home a learning game, manipulative device, file folder activity, or task card to complete.

Send Tasks to the Sick Child. When a child is sick at home and work is requested, put several learning materials in a shopping bag for the learner to complete at home.

SPECIFIC WAYS TO IMPLEMENT CREATIVE LEARNING MATERIALS IN THE HOME

Set Up a Learning Table. Set up a special corner of a room for the child to call his or her own work area. On a small table or desk provide such materials as scissors, crayons, pencils, paste, paper, and a ruler. The child can use this area to work with all types of learning materials.

Specify an Activity Time. Set aside a certain period of time each day to use learning materials with your child. The child will enjoy this special time shared with you and you will gain a better insight into your child's strengths and weaknesses in the various skill areas.

Plan a Game Night. Set aside a certain night each week or month for your child to select a game board to play with other family members. For added variety, have the child design a game board to use with others.

Initiate a Special Project. When your child shows a special interest in a subject or asks questions on a particular topic, provide tasks and activities for the child to complete based on the topic. A special project can also be initiated after taking a trip or visiting a museum or historical site.

Plan a Library Trip. Go to the library with your child and select a book. At home write tasks, based on the book, for her or him to complete.

Plan Activities for Traveling. When traveling, how many times have you heard the questions, "Are we there yet?" or "How much further to go?" Ease the boredom of the tiresome ride by packing a shopping bag with learning materials, paper, crayons, and pencils. These materials will help the hours of travel to fly by. If traveling for an extended period of time, the child can use the learning materials in a hotel or motel room.

Provide Tasks for Holidays or Special Occasions. Around holidays or special occasions there seems to be a feeling of excitement in the air. On task cards write activities for the child to do such as making a holiday art project or writing a creative story.

Provide Tasks for Television Shows. After watching a television show, provide tasks and activities based on the theme of the show. Activities can include writing a short synopsis of the show, listing the main characters, and putting the events of the show in sequence.

SPECIFIC WAYS TO IMPLEMENT CREATIVE LEARNING MATERIALS IN THE COMMUNITY

Use Learning Materials in the Library. The world is at a learner's fingertips through books and the library is just the place to "set the stage" for learning about the many wonders of the world through creative learning materials. Through their use, a child's curiosity and general fund of knowledge can be increased and an appreciation for books and the value of reading can be fostered as well.

To "set the stage" for learning, provide various learning activities, projects, and tasks designed to encourage the child to read books, use references, and research special topics. Task cards can be based on selected books and require the learner to read the story and list the main characters, identify the central theme, sequence the order of events, or tell the story through pictures. Special activities or projects can be provided that encourage the child to look up information about a historical event, celebration, holiday, or special place such as a country, state, or city.

By setting up a special work area, unique and interesting projects can be created. For example, the child can be encouraged to make a mobile or a three-dimensional picture based on a selected storybook or design a puppet of a character from a book.

Whatever the project, task, or activity, the learner is encouraged to use books and read for knowledge and enjoyment.

Use Learning Materials for Club Activities. Whether you work with Scouts or are involved with helping children in other club activities such as cooking, woodworking, arts and crafts, or creative writing, learning materials can be used. In Scouts, activities can be designed to help the children earn various badges. For other club activities, learning materials can be used as a motivating technique or as a follow-up activity.

Depending upon the size of the club, divide the children into small groups. One group can be working with you on a specific project, while other children can be using a game board or other manipulative material independently.

HINTS FOR IMPLEMENTATION

In order to ensure the successful use of learning materials, careful planning and organization is necessary. Factors to consider include setting up a work area, choosing appropriate materials, establishing rules and guidelines, scheduling the use of the materials, and record keeping.

The following list of helpful hints is provided to help you plan and organize the learning environment:

- Set up a work area in a quiet corner of the classroom or home.
- Store learning materials and all necessary supplies such as markers, spinners, dice, paper, pencils, paste, crayons, and rulers in a bookcase or on a table.
- Provide a cover of a box, similar in size to a shirt box, for the learner to put finished work papers in.
- Store markers and dice in a small container, such as a margarine container, so they are readily available for the learner to use.
- Store pencils, paste, crayons, and other supplies in a small basket or dish pan.
- Check the supply area daily to be sure everything is in order and that there are enough supplies.
- Change the tasks in the work area periodically because children like variety and often tire of the same task.
- Establish, with the learner, rules and guidelines necessary to create a happy learning climate. Such rules and guidelines will vary depending upon the setting, but all children should learn to take care of materials, put them away when tasks are completed, and keep the work and supply areas clean.
- Discuss the directions on the learning materials with the learner to be sure that he or she understands what to do.
- Teach a couple of children how to use a learning material that several children are going to use. They, in turn, can teach the others how to use it.
- Arrange special times with the learner to discuss activities she or he has completed independently and also to provide guidance and answer any questions that might arise.
- Arrange a schedule for using the materials. Plan the times so they will not conflict with other activities.
- Mark on a calendar when special projects should be completed.
- Make a chart and for each completed activity give the learner a star or a decorative seal.
- Provide rewards or incentives for completing a special project. Such a reward might be a field trip or choice of a favorite dinner.

TYPES OF LEARNING MATERIALS

The following types of learning materials can be created for any occasion. Each one is presented with a brief discussion of its unique qualities and benefits as well as with an illustrative example. It should be noted that each section of Part Two is devoted to a particular type.

FILE FOLDER ACTIVITIES

File folder activities are learning devices, game boards, or tasks designed on manila or colored file folders. Based on a central theme, each activity is designed to provide skill development, enrichment, or other unique learning opportunity. Included on the file folder are from one to several tasks for the learner to perform. For continuity, each task as well as the various pieces, cards, or parts utilized by the learner to complete the tasks are linked to the central theme. By design, the file folder activity is based on the learner's needs and interests and consequently is motivational to the learner.

The illustration *Digging Up Bones* is an example of a file folder activity. The skill concentration of the activity is the recognition of the hard and soft *c* sound.

File folder activities are attractive, inexpensive to make, and easy to store and organize. Drawings, magazine pictures, stickers, cut-out patterns, or shapes are used to "dress up" the folder. Storage pockets affix easily for activity pieces as well as a slide strip, banner, turning wheel, or pulley.

For descriptions and illustrations of file folder activities see the section titled *Fancy File Folder Activities.*

TASK CARDS

Task cards are learning activities and tasks placed on cards of various sizes and shapes. Standard index or poster board cards and other cards constructed from assorted patterns are used. Usually focused on one skill area or specific skill, each task card is designed to provide reinforcement, practice in application and problem solving, or enrichment experiences. Through colorful and interesting pictures or patterns, intriguing questions and problems, or manipulative devices to use, the learner is motivated and challenged to perform the various tasks. Tasks on the cards are either closed-ended with one specific response or answer required or open-ended with more than one possibility in learner response.

The illustration *Spouting Off Facts* is an example of a Task Card. The specific skill being reinforced is the multiplication facts for the table of *3.*

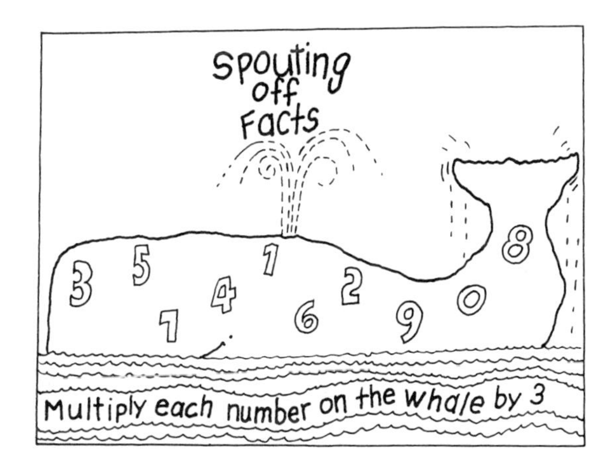

Task cards are easy to construct, use, and store. Storage pockets, slide strips, spinners, wheels, or other manipulative devices may be affixed.

Some different types of task cards include Stand-Up Cross Shaped Task Card, Mobile Task, Box-a-Task, Bookmark Task, Triangular Task, and Attach-a-Task.

For descriptions and illustrations of Task Cards see the section titled *On Task With Task Cards.*

GAME BOARDS

As learning materials, game boards use various courses and plans for skill development and reinforcement. The game course and skills are unified by a central theme along with markers, cards, spinners, and answer keys (where appropriate). Game courses, constructed on poster board, may be spiral, letter, number, vertical, zig-zag, or X-shaped. Skill development and reinforcement is provided by the game plan and/or rules. From one to several players move markers around the course by using a spinner, die, or other movement strategy and answer questions, usually on cards, pertaining to the skill being reinforced. Movements include Forward, Reward (extra turn), Penalty (lose turn or go back space), Short Cuts, and Long-Way Detours.

Game boards may focus on a specific skill or skill area or be multipurpose. A multipurpose game board is one that allows for adjustments or changes in skill concentration. A game board is usually made multipurpose by providing question or fact cards that can be easily changed to meet specific skill needs.

The *Olympic Champ* example illustrates a game board that is multipurpose in design.

Game boards as learning tools are an exciting and challenging approach to use in the motivation of learners for skill development. Unique and interesting patterns, pictures, and cutouts as well as unusual and intriguing moves may be strategically placed to captivate the learner's interest and challenge her or him to perform.

For descriptions and illustrations of Game Boards see the section titled *On the Move With Game Boards.*

MANIPULATIVE DEVICES

Manipulative devices are learning activities and tasks constructed from poster board and/or assorted scrap and junk materials. (See the section titled *A*

Treasure Chest of Scrap and Junk Materials.) Depending upon raw materials available, various games, activities, and tasks are designed to provide skill development, reinforcement, enrichment, or other unique learning opportunity. Based on learner's needs and interest, manipulative devices provide beneficial "hands on" learning experiences that prompt and motivate attention to task and performance.

Under the Big Top is an example of a manipulative device. The skill concentration of the learning material is initial consonant blends.

Manipulative devices are unique, interesting, and exciting learning activities for the designer to create as well as for the learner to utilize for skill development and reinforcement.

For descriptions and illustrations of manipulative devices see the section titled *Manipulative Devices That Matter.*

CHARACTERISTICS THAT MAKE THE DIFFERENCE

The uses and benefits of creative learning materials become increasingly apparent through their many unique characteristics. Depending upon how they will be used and in what setting, the designer should draw upon these characteristics and incorporate some or all of the ideas in the design and development of a material. It is through these characteristics that the differences in learner's interest and needs, resulting in skill attainment and mastery, are more readily realized.

Skill Focused. Each task or activity is focused on one specific skill such as addition facts to sums of eighteen, antonyms, telling time to the hour, measuring to the inch or half-inch, or using selected references.

Motivational. Colorful interesting pictures, shapes, or cutouts as well as activities that often require matching, sorting, identifying, and other things "to do" are highly motivating to the learner. The learner explores and experiences carefully prepared tasks through manipulation.

Individualized. Tasks and activities are individualized to meet specific skill needs as well as individual interest needs. The specific skill is matched with and incorporated into interesting experiences appropriate to the grade, age, and/or social level of the learner.

Based on Student Interest. Timely topics, current events, movies, television programs, hobbies, fascinations, movie characters, important personalities, books, stories, poems, and so on are utilized to increase the learner's interest in the task or activity. Depending upon the interest of the grade or age level as well as individual learner interest, the use of these as themes will increase the learner's motivation, concentration, and attention to the task.

Independent Oriented. By design, tasks and activities are performed independently by the learner. Independent study is prompted through the use of clear and specific directions, comprehensible vocabulary, visual clues, examples or illustrations, and if appropriate or desirable, an answer key in which the learner may check her or his own performance. Thus, the learner is often able to complete the task from beginning to end with little or no assistance.

Adaptable. Tasks and activities are adaptable to a wide variety of skills and skill areas as well as grades and/or age levels. Questions or tasks may be adjusted, simplified, or made more difficult. Also, the interest level may be readily adjusted by changes in the activity theme, that is, the pictures used or characters presented may be changed to meet learner's needs and interest.

Manipulative. Most tasks are "hands on" for the learner and use such techniques and devices as spinners, pulleys, puzzles to complete, or objects to assemble. The learner *sorts, places, matches, inserts, spins, fastens, opens,* and so on, to perform the various tasks.

Self-Checkable. By design, tasks and activities are self-checkable. In addition to a wide variety of answer keys in various shapes and sizes, success on tasks may be assured the learner by completing a puzzle, figuring out a code or secret message, or using all of a certain color item as a part of the task.

Durable. By laminating or using clear adhesive paper to cover and protect the material, it becomes long-lasting and is utilized over and over by many learners. As is possible, parts and pieces are attached to or stored in envelopes or pockets affixed to the material.

DESIGNING LEARNING MATERIALS

A STEP-BY-STEP APPROACH

The design and development of learning materials requires careful planning, organization, and considerations. The designer must acquire certain specific information about the learner regarding skill needs and interest; then, he or she must lay out and plan the activity, gathering the raw materials; and finally, he or she must put it all together, adapting and adjusting when necessary. If materials are to be useful and consequently, successful learning tools, careful planning is required throughout. The following step-by-step approach is provided as a guide to use in the design of learning materials, and as such, each step provides important points to consider, techniques to use, and questions to ask in the design and construction of the material.

A STEP-BY-STEP APPROACH FOR DESIGNING LEARNING MATERIALS

Step 1: Gather Information about the Learner
Step 2: Specify the Skill and Purpose
Step 3: Select a Theme
Step 4: Plan, Lay Out, and Construct the Material
Step 5: State the Task
Step 6: Evaluate

Step 1 Gather Information About the Learner

In addition to age, grade level and placement, and general subject area, more specific information about the learner is necessary. What are the learner's *specific strengths* (what he/she can do)? What are the learner's *specific weaknesses* (what he/she cannot do)? What skills does the learner know how to perform, need more practice in, or not know? Consideration must also be given to identifying ways in which the learner *learns best.* Some prefer seeing (visual) tasks, others hearing (auditory) tasks. Task preference may also range from the *concrete* with specific responses required, to *abstract* with more open-ended-type questions.

What *interests* and *motivates* the learner is also important to identify. Favorite hobbies, sports, games, movies, books, television shows, and characters should be explored as well as clubs, organizations (such as Girl Scouts, Boy Scouts), and summer experiences the learner enjoys.

The following list suggests some techniques to use in gathering information about the learner.

Techniques to Use in Gathering Information about the Learner

1. *Student Records.* Look over student records in school, noting skills mastered, special interests and achievements, and test results. Pay special attention to specific strengths and weaknesses.
2. *Communicate with Teacher(s).* Discuss with current and/or previous teacher(s) the learner's skill concentration and focus, special interests, and types of activities and tasks preferred.
3. *Question the Learner.* Perhaps the best source of information is the learner. Ask specific questions regarding likes and dislikes, types of tasks and activities preferred, and special interests and experiences.
4. *Parent/Teacher Conferences.* Share and gain information about the learner frequently through regularly scheduled conferences. It is beneficial to discover areas of study, skill focus, special interests, and current happenings.
5. *Report Card(s).* Current and previous report cards provide much information about school performance, strong and weak subject areas, and work habits.
6. *Communicate with Learner's Peers.* Peers within the school and/or neighborhood can be helpful and resourceful regarding special interests and experiences.
7. *Observation.* Observe the learner in school, home, or community. Note attention to tasks, concentration, work/study/play habits, special interests, projects, games, and activities.
8. *Give Formal and Informal Tests.* If you are a teacher, give formal diagnostic test or teacher-constructed informal test. Choose or design one that will clearly indicate specific strengths and weaknesses in the particular skill area.

Questions to Ask in Gathering Information about the Learner

1. What are the learner's specific strengths (what does he/she know)?
2. What are the learner's specific weaknesses (what does he/she not know or need reinforcement in)?

3. How does the learner learn best?
4. What will interest and motivate the learner?
5. What types of activities or projects does the learner enjoy doing?

Step 2
Specify the Skill and Purpose

Learning materials are useful and beneficial for the

- introduction of a new skill,
- drill and reinforcement of a skill,
- application of a previously learned skill.

Specify the Skill. Regardless of the use, the skill as well as the purpose must be specified. Upon identifying the learner's specific strengths and weaknesses as suggested in Step 1, the specific skill area requiring attention should be pointed out. It is necessary, however, to further specify or break down the skill area and clearly identify the specific skill. The specific skill will then become the skill concentration of the learning material. The following list presents illustrative examples:

Skill Area	*Specific Skill*
Phonics	initial consonant *l* blends
Phonics	syllabication
Language	abbreviations
Mathematics	subtraction with renaming (borrowing)
Mathematics	telling time to the half hour

Specify the Purpose. Once the skill has been specified, it is important to clearly identify and indicate the purpose of the learning material.

The purpose is the performance objective of the learner. It reflects the specific skill in terms of what the learner will do or be able to do by using the material.

Based upon the specific skill identified, the purpose further defines in specific terms the action required of the learner through the use of the material.

Included with the preceding skill areas and specific skills identified as example for each, the following purposes are presented to illustrate:

Skill Area	*Specific Skill*	*Purpose*
Phonics	initial consonant *l* blends	The learner will be able to form words by matching the *l* blends, (*bl, sl, fl, gl, cl, pl*) to an ending sound.
Phonics	syllabication	Given a list of words, the learner will be able to determine the number of syllables in each word.
Language	abbreviations	The learner will be able to match the abbreviations of a word to the word it represents.
Mathematics	subtraction with renaming (borrowing)	Given subtraction examples, the learner will be able to subtract hundreds, tens, and ones with renaming.
Mathematics	telling time to the half hour	Given a specific time, the learner will be able to set a clock to the half hour.

Questions to Ask in Specifying the Skill and Purpose

1. What is the skill area?
2. Has the skill area been sufficiently broken down to a specific skill?
3. What is the specific skill?
4. Is the skill to be introduced, reinforced, or applied?
5. What is the purpose?

Step 3
Select a Theme

Consistency in design and character of the learning material is set by a central theme. The theme can be as broad and general as "outer space" or as specific as a particular cartoon character. The theme helps to establish unity in the various components of the material. Pictures and characters used are linked with, and incorporated into, tasks, projects, and activities.

When selecting a theme, always keep in mind learner *interest.* Choose a theme that is appropriate for the age, grade, and social level of the learner, and most importantly, one that will interest and motivate him/her to perform. Good resources for theme selection are movies, hobbies, children's books, timely topics, current events, fads, holidays, historical events, television shows/characters, familiar sites in the community, animals, pets, sports, nature, and general areas of interest such as outer space and the circus.

Questions to Ask in Selecting a Theme

1. What theme will interest the learner?
2. Will the theme motivate the learner to perform?
3. Is the theme appropriate for the age, grade, and social level of the learner?
4. Will the theme allow for unity and consistency of the various components within the material?

Step 4
Plan, Lay Out, and Construct the Material

Once the specific skill and purpose are identified and a theme has been selected, the designer is now ready to plan, lay out, and construct the learning material.

Depending on learner and/or designer preference and also raw materials gathered or available, the type of learning material will fall into one of the following categories:

- File Folder Activity
- Task Card
- Game Board
- Manipulative Device

(Each of these four types is defined and discussed within the section, *Types of Learning Materials.*)

Regardless of the type of learning material to be constructed, the designer must take care to plan and lay out material. The organization and consistency in construction will ultimately increase the learner's independence, performance, and success with the material.

The following are important elements to consider when planning, laying out, and constructing learning materials.

Unity in Design. Based on the central theme, be it a current popular movie or a special holiday, the various components of the learning material such as title, directions, questions, tasks, and so on should be unified in design throughout. Also, to enhance the material's design, include a spinner or answer key as well as various markers, cards, stickers, unique objects, and devices that are coordinated or linked with the central theme.

Attractiveness in Appearance. Each component within the learning material should be attractive to the learner. By using colorful and interesting pictures, patterns, and devices as well as neatness and organization in presentation, the learner's motivation, interest, and attention to the task is increased.

Here presented are several hints for enhancing the appearance of the learning material:

- Include a "catchy" title based on the theme, presented in bold or block lettering.
- Use stickers, decals, and unique objects within the design.
- Use markers or pens of various colors.
- Provide a unique answer key.
- Use interesting and unique storage pockets.
- Use special devices such as a spinner, turning wheel, pulley, or slide.
- Section off each task or series of tasks.
- Number or letter the order of tasks.

Compactness and Durability. The constructed learning material should be compact and durable throughout. Activity pieces, markers, dice, spinner, and any other device should be affixed to or stored within the material. By doing so, the learning material will contain within and of itself most of the necessary tools or pieces needed by the learner to complete the task. Also, to promote easy and long-lasting use, make the complete learning material including the pieces, cards, markers, spinner, answer key, and any other device durable. This can be done by laminating or using clear self-adhesive paper to cover the material.

Questions to Ask in Planning, Laying Out, and Constructing the Material

1. What type of learning material (File Folder Activity, Task Card, Game Board, Manipulative Device) is preferred?
2. What raw materials are available? Needed?
3. Are the various components organized and consistent with the theme and specific skill?
4. Are all the pieces of the activity affixed or stored on the material, including markers, spinners, cards, and other devices needed for the activity?
5. Is the material compact, durable, and safe?

Step 5
State the Task

To increase learner independence, concentration, motivation, and success on the activity, tasks should be stated in order, with clarity, and should provide visual clues.

Order. Order the tasks on the activity in sequence or steps regarding which the learner is to do first, second, third, and so on. Standard numbering (1, 2, 3) or lettering (A, B, C) are useful for this. To order tasks by degree of difficulty or to break up or section off tasks, use different-colored pens or markers in addition to drawing lines or boxes around the task. In any event, order the tasks clearly for the learner to follow and understand what she or he is *to do* and in *what sequence.*

Clarity. Clarity in stating the task, being specific about what the learner is *to do* and *how* he or she is to do it will increase learner performance and attention. In doing so, use words and terminology the learner knows and understands and avoid lengthy statements, rules, or directions. The task directions should be *brief* and *to the point.*

Visual Clues. Visual clues, such as pictures, illustrations, examples, signs, and symbols will enhance the material and increase learner independence and motivation. Photographs, pictures, charts, shapes, and designs, accompanied by directional arrows and visual markers will emphasize to the learner the task to perform and/or how it is performed.

Questions to Ask in Stating the Task

1. What task(s) or activity is the learner to do?
2. Will the learner understand specifically what she or he is to do?
3. Are the tasks or steps of the activity in a sequenced order?
4. Is the learner able to read and understand the tasks?
5. Are the directions for the task brief and to the point?
6. Are visual clues provided?

Step 6
Evaluate

Learner performance on the learning material, including skill mastery, improvement, or the need for additional reinforcement of the skill is assured through evaluation. Evaluation indicates the success level of the learner, and consequently, the direction of the teaching/learning process. As is indicated through evaluation, additional drill and reinforcement may be necessary or the skill is mastered and therefore a new skill is to be presented.

As well as assuring learner performance and skill information to the instructor, evaluation provides necessary feedback to the learner regarding performance and success. Prompt or immediate feedback is best for it will clearly indicate to the learner how well the task has been performed and/or what improvements are necessary.

Three methods for evaluating learner performance on learning materials are *Teacher-check, Peer-check,* and *Learner-check.*

Teacher-Check

Completed tasks and activities are checked by the teacher for accuracy, completeness, and overall performance. As stated in the task directions, the learner is required to complete a specific written or manipulative assignment as a part of the activity. Learner's written assignments may include responding to the task questions on paper, worksheets or cutout object papers coordinated with the task. Manipulative tasks may be checked immediately or soon after learner completion. Keep in mind that as the learner is performing the task, ongoing input from the instructor is helpful and reinforcing to the learner.

Feedback to the learner, either written or verbal, should be positive, provide reinforcement, and most of all, be personalized.Let the learner know *frequently* that you are pleased with his/her performance on the task.

Peer-check

A peer of the learner may check task completion, skill accuracy, and learner performance. Pairing off learners, providing one with an answer key, will allow for immediate feedback on skill attainment as well as create a cooperative, "helping" learning environment. An older learner may be selected to act as a "tutor," thereby providing the learner with ongoing support and reinforcement throughout the learning activity.

Learner-check

To provide immediate reinforcement and increase learner independence, tasks and activities are designed to be learner-checkable. This may be accomplished in several ways depending on the particular task or activity. Techniques to use in making tasks or activities learner-checkable include:

Coding. Task answers are numbered or letter-coded to spell out a message, phrase, word, or to complete a design.

Puzzles. Puzzle pieces will only match and/or join appropriately with the correct answer.

Dot-to-Dot. A dot-to-dot is coordinated with task answers. The learner completes the dot-to-dot by correctly performing the task.

Answer Key. An answer key is provided the learner to self-check performance. The answer key may be a separate card or paper with the correct responses or it may be affixed to the activity.

Questions to Ask in Evaluating

1. How well has the learner performed the task?
2. Is additional drill and reinforcement of the skill necessary?
3. Has the learner mastered the skill?
4. Has the learner been provided with feedback (verbal or written)?
5. Is the feedback immediate or does it come soon after the task is completed?
6. Was the learner able to perform and check the task independently?

TECHNIQUES TO USE IN CONSTRUCTION

The following section provides many tips and techniques to use in the construction of learning materials. Most are applicable to any of the four types of materials presented—File Folder Activities, Task Cards, Game Boards, and Manipulative Devices.

Markers

Buttons. Buttons of various colors, sizes, and shapes are good to use.

Plastic Toys. Small plastic toys such as airplanes or cars can be used.

Milk or Bottle Caps. Use milk or bottle caps of different colors.

Coins. Use a penny, dime, or nickel.

Stickers or Seals. Stickers or seals stuck on small pieces of poster board can be used.

Thread Spools. Use empty thread spools of different sizes.

Marker Caps. Indelible marker caps of various colors can be used.

Spinners and Dice

Paper Clip Spinner. Insert a paper brad through a paper clip and attach it to the center of a small poster board square or disc. Divide it into sections and write a number in each.

Paper Plate Spinner. Attach a paper clip spinner to a small paper plate.

Lid Spinner. Attach a paper clip spinner to the center of a coffee can or margarine lid.

Box Die. Cover a small square box with plain wrapping or self-adhesive paper. Write numbers on each side to form the die.

Sponge Dice. Make quiet dice by cutting cubes from a sponge.

Pockets

Storage Pockets. From construction paper or poster board cut out pocket shapes of various sizes. Glue three sides of each cutout pocket shape onto a learning material and use them to store game pieces or cards. Cover the pockets with clear self-adhesive paper to make them durable. Use the edge of a scissor to slit the top of each pocket to form an opening.

Object Pocket. Use cutout objects such as animals or flowers to make pockets on the activity.

Mini-Pockets. Paste several mini-pockets on the learning material for the learner to place answer cards.

Cloth Pockets. Make pockets using scraps of cloth and affix to the activity.

Manila or String-Tie Envelope. Affix a manila or string-tie envelope to a learning material to store pieces and/or cards. (It is recommended that string-tie envelopes be used instead of manila envelopes. The fasteners on manila envelopes often break with continual use.)

Unique Devices

Spin-a-Tub. Put the spinner for a game on the lid of a margarine tub or coffee can and store the pieces of the game inside.

Yarn Match. Use yarn to match items.

Turning Wheel. Cut two wheels of different sizes from poster board. Put the smaller wheel on top of the larger and attach it with a paper brad in the middle. This can also be made with one wheel (circle) attached to the middle of a piece of poster board.

Puzzle Format. Draw a simple object on poster board or use a mounted magazine picture. Cut it into several pieces to make a puzzle.

Slide Strip. A narrow strip of poster board acts as a slide as it moves up and down between two slits on the material.

Yarn Pulley. Cut two slits several inches apart on the activity. Put yarn through the two slits and tie it in the back to make the pulley.

Game Courses

Spiral Course. Draw a spiral on a round piece of poster board or on a pizza disc to form the course.

Letter Course. Use a letter of the alphabet to form the course.

Number Course. Use a single digit number to form a course for a game.

Vertical Course. Several vertical courses can be drawn on one game board. Each player playing the game uses one course.

Zig-Zag Course. A game course in a zig-zag design can be used.

Calendar Course. One or more old calendar pages can be used as a course.

Sticker Course. Holiday or object stickers can be used as a game course.

Coding Label Dot Course. Arrange coding label dots to form a course.

Answer Keys

Answer Flap. Write answers on a learning material and paste a construction paper flap over them. After the activity is completed, the learner lifts the flap to find the answers. The answer flap may be made square, rectangular, or object-shaped.

Answer Key. Write answers for the activity on an index card or on an object-shaped card that is based on the theme of the activity.

Answers on Back. Write the answers on the back of the learning material.

Answers on Game Cards. Answers are written on the back of game cards.

Decorative Cutouts

Wallpaper Scraps or Samples. Use pictures cut from wallpaper scraps or sample books to decorate learning materials or to cover file folders.

Pizza Cardboard Discs. Use these for learning wheel activities or game boards.

Calendars. Use the numbers on old calendars instead of writing numbers.

Photographs. Photographs of familiar objects or places such as pets, children, or historical sites can be used on learning activities.

Wrapping Paper. Use sheets of paper to cover file folders or cutouts from the paper to decorate the materials.

Paper Tablecloths. Cut out objects from tablecloths to use on learning materials.

Newspapers. Decorate learning materials with specific sections from the newspaper (sports, weather, classified).

Magazine Pictures. Choose pictures of interest to the learner to decorate learning materials.

Special Tools

Grease Pencil. This pencil (available in an office supply store) can be used to write on any laminated or self-adhesive covered surface. It will wipe off with a damp cloth.

Lamination or Clear Self-Adhesive Paper. Get as much use from your learning activities as possible by protecting them with either clear self-adhesive paper or lamination. When applying self-adhesive paper, prick any bubbles that appear on the surface with a pin to smooth them out. For materials with slits or cuts use clear self-adhesive paper instead of lamination. When trimming, leave at least an eighth of an inch as a border around laminated materials.

A TREASURE CHEST OF SCRAP AND JUNK MATERIALS

Start a scrap and junk collection. Search through every closet, cabinet, drawer, and wastebasket for the variety of everyday items or scrap and junk materials that will be worth their "weight in gold" as you construct learning materials. With a little imagination and creativity, these easy-to-find items can change plain learning materials into attractive and innovative ones.

The reasons and possibilities that prompt the use of these materials are as endless as the diversity of items themselves. These "treasures" are the raw materials that can be uniquely used for and within the design of learning materials. Some items can be used to decorate the learning materials and others to create special devices or activity pieces. Additional items can also be used as game markers or for storage. Whatever the use, these items will be invaluable to you in the construction of learning materials.

Get children involved in the search for the scrap and junk materials. Plan a treasure-chest hunt to see who can find the most items for the "treasure chest" (storage box).

The following list is a collection of scrap and junk materials to get you started in filling your "treasure chest." It is suggested that as additional items are discovered, they be added to the list.

bleach bottles	bottle caps	buttons
coat hangers	coffee cans	catalogs
cotton balls	clothespins	cereal (alphabet)
greeting cards	egg cartons	felt

feathers
key rings
magazines
magazine pictures
pipe cleaners
styrofoam packing
tennis ball cans
wallpaper
burlap
coloring books
muffin tins
indelible marker caps
shoe laces
cigar boxes
cigarette boxes
shoe boxes
tabs from cans
straw baskets
carpet samples
sample tile squares
picture hanger hooks
shells
velcro
automobile sales catalogs
supermarket flyers
wrapping paper
paper tablecloth
fake fur
material remnants
margarine containers
postcards
ribbon
thread spools
cardboard tubes
wooden beads
clothesline
detergent bottles
magnets
yarn
plastic bags
envelopes
instant soup boxes
food labels
oatmeal containers
styrofoam meat trays
aluminum foil
milk jugs
pine cones
seeds
washers
detergent boxes
manila envelopes
writing paper boxes
coffee can lids
juice cans
maps
newspapers
paper plates
string
travel brochures
wire
zippers
cups (styrofoam, paper)
macaroni
milk cartons
sponges
candy boxes
glitter
popsicle sticks
pizza discs
lima beans
corn
rubber jar rings
paper bags
socks
nylon stockings
window shades
bread fasteners (square)
old workbooks
paper placemats
plastic straws

HINTS FOR ORGANIZATION AND STORAGE

ORGANIZATION

File Folder Activities

Color Code. Use folders of different colors for specific subject areas or skills. (Examples: green—math; yellow—reading; blue—science)

Writing on Tabs. Write on the tabs with particular colored marker for specific areas or skills.

Dot on Tab. With selected colors, make a dot with a marker or use a coding label dot to code folders according to subjects or skills.

Number on Tab. Number folders according to subject area or by skills. (Examples: 1—50, math; 51—100, reading; 1—25, addition; 26—50, subtraction)

Letter/Number Code. Use the first letter of the subject or skill area with a number in sequence after it to code file folders. (Examples: Reading—R–1, R–2, R–3, etc; Math—M–1, M–2, M–3, etc.)

Star on Tab. Use self-adhesive stars of various colors to code specific subject areas or skills.

Labels for Tabs. Use commercial labels for tabs and code folders according to color of tab.

Task Cards, Game Boards, and Manipulative Devices

Dot Code. With selected colors, make a dot with a marker or use a coding label dot to code learning materials according to subject area or skill.

Number Code. Number learning materials according to subject area or by skill.

Color-Coded Writing. Write the titles of learning materials with a specific colored marker according to subject area or skill.

Poster Board Code. Use poster board of different colors for specific subject areas or skills. (Examples: green—math; yellow—reading)

Shape Code. Draw a geometric shape on learning materials for specific subject areas or skills. (Examples: square—math; triangle—reading)

Learning Materials Directory. A directory of all creative materials should be kept in a loose leaf notebook for easy reference. List materials according to subject area or skill.

STORAGE

Detergent or Cereal Boxes. Cut off the tops of large detergent or cereal boxes and cover with patterned self-adhesive paper. Store file folder activities or task cards in these boxes.

Portable File. An inexpensive desk top file can be purchased to store file folder activities and task cards.

Cigarette Boxes or Instant Soup Boxes. When covered with self-adhesive paper, these boxes make great storage for small games.

Shoe Boxes. Several small games can be stored in a shoe box. When covered with different colors of self-adhesive paper, boxes can be used for specific subject areas or skills.

Plastic Bags. Store game parts in plastic bags and clip to game board with a clothespin.

Metal Band Aid Box or Stationery Box. These boxes are good for storage of small games.

Margarine Tubs. Store game markers and pieces in margarine containers.

Manila Envelopes. Store small learning games or activities in a manila envelope. For larger games, store pieces or parts in a manila envelope and affix to learning material.

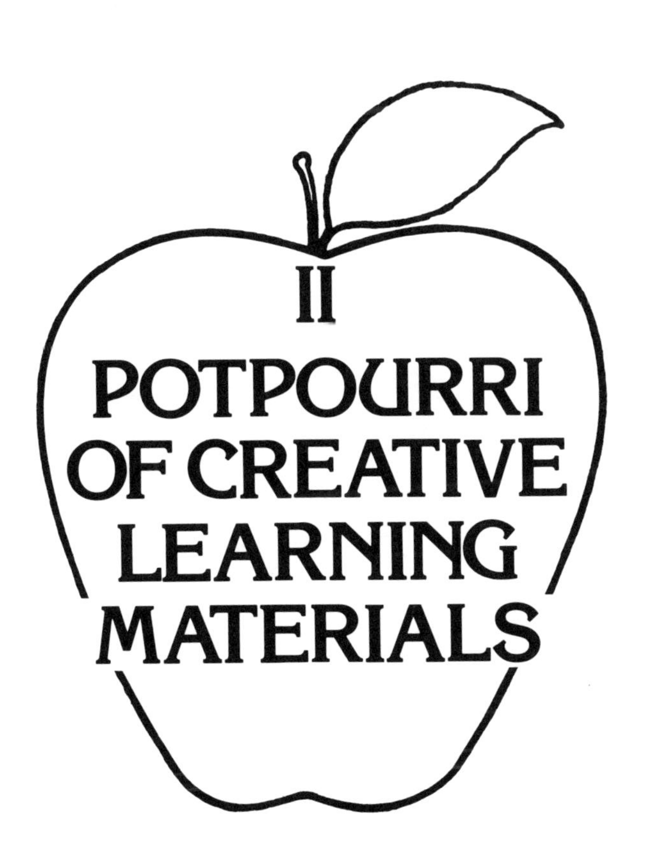
II
POTPOURRI
OF CREATIVE
LEARNING
MATERIALS

FANCY FILE FOLDER ACTIVITIES

FERRIS WHEEL SPIN

SKILL: Initial Consonant Blends—*l*

PURPOSE: The learner will be able to form words by matching the *l* blends (*bl, sl, fl, gl, cl, pl*) to an ending sound.

Note: A *consonant blend* is formed when two or more consonants are together and each sound is heard.

MATERIALS: File folder, poster board (12″ × 18″), paper brad.

CONSTRUCTION OF FOLDER: On the cover, illustrate and color a ticket stand and a large banner.

Cut two circles, one 7″ and the other 5″, from the poster board. Draw a ferris wheel with seats on the larger circle and in each seat write an *l* blend (*bl, sl, fl, gl, cl, pl*). Divide the smaller circle into six to eight evenly spaced sections and write an incomplete word in each.

Sample incomplete words include:

__y	__ocks	__ane
__own	__ide	__at
__ed	__ate	__ope

Inside the folder, on the right side, attach the circles, smaller centered on larger, with a paper brad.

Write the directions for the folder on the side opposite the ferris wheel.

DIRECTIONS ON FOLDER: Spin the circles to form new words. Write the words on paper.

ADDITIONAL ACTIVITIES: Think of and list words associated with an amusement park that have a blend in them.

Other folders, similar in design, can be constructed by making additional circles and using words with *s* or *r* blends.

HERE'S THE PITCH

SKILL: Consonant Digraphs—*th, sh, wh, ch.*

PURPOSE: The learner will be able to form words by selecting the correct consonant digraph (*th, sh, wh, ch*).

Note: A *consonant digraph* is made up of two consonants that come together and make one sound.

MATERIALS: File folder, construction paper, baseball cards and/or pictures, string-tie envelope.

CONSTRUCTION OF FOLDER: Draw four baseballs, approximately 3″ in diameter, on the inside of the folder and write a consonant digraph (*th, sh, wh, ch*) on each.

Make twenty-five small cutout baseball bats and on each bat write an incomplete word.

Sample incomplete words include:

th	*sh*	*wh*	*ch*
__ird	__ort	__eat	__ild

__ink	__ould	__ip	__ange
__ank	__ave	__y	__op
__irst	__ine	__en	__ick
__ing	__ell	__ite	__ain

From construction paper, cut out a baseball and write the answers on it to use as an answer key. Store bats and baseball answer key in a string-tie envelope attached to the back of the folder.

Decorate the rest of the folder with baseball cards or pictures.

DIRECTIONS ON FOLDER: What kind of pitcher are you? Take the bats out of the envelope on the back. Look at the incomplete word on each and decide what consonant digraph is needed to make a word. Place the bat on the correct baseball. Check your work with the baseball answer key when you have finished.

ADDITIONAL ACTIVITIES: List words associated with the sport of baseball that have a digraph in them.

Use a mirror to observe the placement of the tongue and lips as each digraph is said.

On a tape recorder, record the digraph sounds in isolation, along with several words containing each, for the learner to hear.

PACK YOUR BAGS

SKILL: Dictionary Usage—Guide Words

PURPOSE: The learner will be able to sort words alphabetically using guide words.

Note: The first and last entry words on each page of a dictionary are *guide words.*

MATERIALS: File folder, poster board (12″ × 18″), travel brochures, clear self-adhesive paper, grease pencil, string-tie envelope.

CONSTRUCTION OF FOLDER: Paste pictures from travel brochures on the cover of the file folder.

Inside, draw two open suitcases. Cover the folder with clear self-adhesive paper or laminate. Use a dictionary to find guide words and with a grease pencil write two guide words at the top of each suitcase.

From poster board cut out about sixteen 2″ × 3″ cards and on each write a word that can be found on the same page as the guide words.

Sample guide words and words for cards include:

cap—carbon		*ceiling—central*	
capable	captain	celebrate	cement
cape	capture	celery	census
capital	car	cell	cent
capsule	caramel	cellar	center

Write answers on a card in the shape of a suitcase. Store cards and answer key in a string-tie envelope attached to the back of the folder.

DIRECTIONS ON FOLDER: Pack your bags by putting the cards in the correct suitcase. To do this, look at the guide words at the top of each suitcase. Read each word on the cards and place in the correct suitcase. Check your answers with the answer key when you have finished.

ADDITIONAL ACTIVITIES: Use a dictionary to look up the following travel words: *airport, passport, conductor, itinerary,* and *tickets.* Write the guide words for the specific word on paper.

Provide additional practice in this skill by changing the guide words and making additional sets of cards.

PICK OF THE CROP

SKILL: Vocabulary Development—Multipurpose

PURPOSE: The learner will be able to increase vocabulary by completing selected tasks.

MATERIALS: File folder, seed catalog, or empty seed packets.

CONSTRUCTION OF FOLDER: Cut and paste vegetable and/or fruit pictures from seed catalogs and/or seed packets on the cover of the folder.

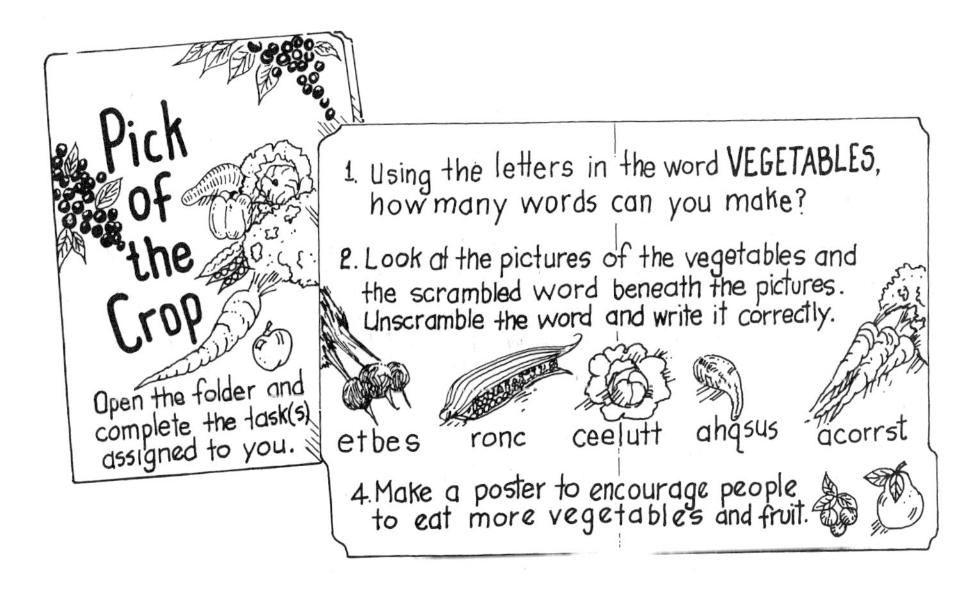

Inside, write tasks pertaining to vegetables or fruit. Sample tasks include:

- Using the letters in the word *vegetables,* how many words can you make?
- Look at the pictures of the vegetables and the scrambled word beneath the pictures. Unscramble the word and write it correctly.
- Imagine that you are a particular fruit or vegetable. Write a story about your life.
- Make a poster to encourage people to eat more vegetables and fruit.

Each task can be written in a different color. This will enable you to assign different tasks to different children or to assign tasks by color for a certain day of the week.

Directions on Folder: Open the folder and complete the task(s) assigned to you.

Additional Activities: Keep a chart of daily eating habits.

Plan a well-balanced diet for one week using foods from the four food groups—meat, milk, fruit/vegetables, and bread/cereal.

Take a shopping trip to a supermarket or farmer's market and have the learner identify the vegetables and fruit.

Provide the learner with soil, pots, and seeds to plant and watch the "pick of the crop" grow.

THE MIDNIGHT RIDE OF PAUL REVERE

SKILL: Creative Writing—Multipurpose

PURPOSE: To be able to write a creative story based on a historical or current event.

MATERIALS: File folder, poster board (9″ × 12″), magazine or other pictures, construction paper, white shelf paper.

CONSTRUCTION OF FOLDER: Decorate the inside and outside of the folder with pictures of Paul Revere's Ride or other important event.

Write tasks or questions relating to the pictures on 4″ × 5″ cards and number each card.

Sample tasks include:

- Imagine that you lived during the time of Paul Revere and that you went on his famous ride with him. Write a story of your adventures. Use a roll of shelf paper to draw a series of pictures to go with your story.
- From the pictures, think of words to make a "Word Search" activity. Use at least twenty words.

Glue a construction paper pocket to the back of the folder to store activity cards.

DIRECTIONS ON FOLDER: Complete the task(s) assigned to you by using the pictures on this folder.

ADDITIONAL ACTIVITIES: Use reference materials to answer the following questions about the event. When and where did the event take place? Why is this event important? Who was involved in the event? What happened during the event?

Write a play about the historical event and then act it out with friends.

Pretend to be a newspaper reporter and write a newspaper articie about the event.

Make additional folders for other historical or current events.

POLLY WANTS A CRACKER

SKILL: Antonyms

PURPOSE: The learner will be able to identify and match word opposites.
Note: Antonyms are words that are opposite in meaning.

MATERIALS: File folder, poster board (9″ × 12″), magazine pictures, string-tie envelope.

CONSTRUCTION OF FOLDER: On the cover, draw or paste a picture of a parrot.

Inside, draw six or eight small parrots and on each parrot write a word that is an opposite (antonym).

Sample antonyms include:

dark—light	big—small	round—square	good—bad
night—day	old—young	weak—strong	first—last

From the poster board cut out six to eight 2″ × 3″ cracker shapes and on each write a word that is the antonym for the one on the parrot. Cut out a larger cracker shape (4″ × 5″) and write the answers on it.

Store crackers and answer key in a string-tie envelope attached to the back of the folder.

DIRECTIONS ON FOLDER: Feed the parrots the crackers by matching the word on the cracker with the word on the parrot that is opposite in meaning. Place the cracker next to the correct parrot.

ADDITIONAL ACTIVITIES: Draw pictures to depict the antonyms.

Think of and list other antonyms.

FACE RACE

SKILL: Punctuation—Period, Question Mark, Exclamation Point

PURPOSE: To be able to select the correct punctuation mark that is placed at the end of a sentence.

Note: A *period* is placed at the end of a telling sentence or one that gives an order or direction. Place a *question mark* at the end of an asking sentence. An *exclamation point* is placed at the end of a sentence that shows strong feeling.

MATERIALS: File folder, poster board (12″ × 18″), magazine pictures, felt remnants, string-tie envelope.

CONSTRUCTION OF FOLDER: Place a large magazine picture of a person with a funny face on the cover.

Inside the folder draw two large heads without the features. From felt remnants, draw and cut out two sets of eyes, ears, eyebrows, nose, mouth, and hair.

Make a set of twenty-five cards and on each card write a sentence without the punctuation mark at the end. On the back of each card write the punctuation mark.

Store cards and face pieces in a string-tie envelope affixed to the back of the folder. Write the directions on the envelope.

DIRECTIONS ON FOLDER: (two players) Be the first to make a funny face. Take cards and face pieces out of the envelope and then open the folder. Choose a head. Place cards, sentence side up. In turn, read the sentence and tell the punctuation mark that should be at the end. Check by turning the card over. If correct, add a part to your face. The first player to complete a face by putting two eyes, a nose, a mouth, two ears, two eyebrows, and hair on the head is the winner.

ADDITIONAL ACTIVITIES: Write sentences using periods, question marks, and exclamation points.

Use the folder to give practice in other kinds of punctuation marks such as commas, quotation marks, and semi-colons. Make a set of cards containing sentences using these punctuation marks.

HOP TO IT

SKILL: Sentences—Question and Telling

PURPOSE: Given a selected group of sentences, the learner will be able to recognize the difference between question and telling sentences.

Note: A *question* is a sentence that asks something and ends in a question mark. A telling sentence is a sentence that tells something and ends in a period.

MATERIALS: File folder, construction paper.

CONSTRUCTION OF FOLDER: On the cover, paste a large lily pad construction paper pocket with a frog on it. This is used to store six to eight cutout frogs, each containing a question or telling sentence.

Inside, paste or draw six or eight lily pads. On each lily pad write *question* or *telling sentence.* Decorate the rest of the folder with other forms of pond life.

DIRECTIONS ON FOLDER: Take the frogs out of the lily pad on the cover and read each sentence on the frogs. Decide whether it is a question or telling sentence and place it on the correct lily pad.

ADDITIONAL ACTIVITIES: Write the sentences on the frogs correctly by adding the correct punctuation mark.

Name the frog on the cover and then write a story about the frog, using questions and telling sentences.

Prepare a list of questions about pond life and then have the learner use reference materials to locate the answers.

SHOOTING STARS

SKILL: Nouns and Verbs

PURPOSE: Given a selected group of words, the learner will be able to recognize the difference between words that are nouns and words that are verbs.

Note: A *noun* is a word that names a person, place or thing. A verb is a word that shows action or is a word of being.

MATERIALS: File folder, construction paper.

CONSTRUCTION OF FOLDER: Cut two large construction paper stars and paste one on each side of the inside of the folder. Label the center of one star *noun* and the other star *verb.*

From construction paper cut ten to twelve small stars and on each write a word that is a noun or a verb.

On the corner of the folder write the answers and put a construction paper flap over them.

On the cover past another large star leaving the top open to store the small stars.

DIRECTIONS ON FOLDER: Take the stars out of the pocket on the front of the folder. If the word on the star is a noun, put it near the star with the word *noun* on it. If the word is a verb, put it near the star with the word *verb* on it. After you have finished, lift the answer flap to check your work.

ADDITIONAL ACTIVITIES: Write a sentence for each word on the small stars.

Draw two stars and label them *noun* and *verb*. In the stars write words associated with space that are nouns or verbs.

Draw or find a picture of outer space and have the learner think of nouns and verbs associated with the picture.

SHOWER POWER

SKILL: Consonant Sounds—Hard and Soft *g*

PURPOSE: To be able to recognize the hard and soft *g* sounds in words.

Note: When the letter *g* is followed by *e, i,* or *y,* it usually has a soft sound similar to the sound of *j*. When *g* is not followed by *e, i,* or *y,* it usually has a hard sound.

MATERIALS: File folder, construction paper.

CONSTRUCTION OF FOLDER: On the cover, paste a construction-paper umbrella and leave an opening in the top to form a pocket. Write the directions on the umbrella and add raindrops around the umbrella.

Inside, draw two large brightly colored umbrellas and label one *Hard g* and the other *Soft g.*

From construction paper make fifteen to twenty raindrops and on each raindrop write words containing *hard g* or *soft g.*

Sample words include:

Hard g		*Soft g*	
game	dog	giant	bridge
dragon	good	package	engine
bag	gate	giraffe	orange
log	glass	huge	gym
gold	goose	gem	gentle

Write answers on a large paper raindrop and use it as an answer key. Store all raindrops in the pocket umbrella on the cover.

Directions on Folder: Take the raindrops out of the umbrella and open the folder. If the word on the raindrop has a *hard g,* put it next to the umbrella with the *Hard g.* If the word on the raindrop has a *soft g,* put it next to the umbrella with the *Soft g.* Check your work when you have finished.

Additional Activities: Find a poem or story about rain. On a large paper raindrop identify and write several *hard g* and *soft g* words from it.

Listen to a song with rain as its theme and identify the *hard g* and *soft g* words.

SYLLABLE MATCH

Skill: Syllabication—1, 2, 3 Syllable Words

Purpose: Given a list of words, the learner will be able to determine the number of syllables in each word.

Note: A *syllable* is a word or part of a word that contains a vowel sound.

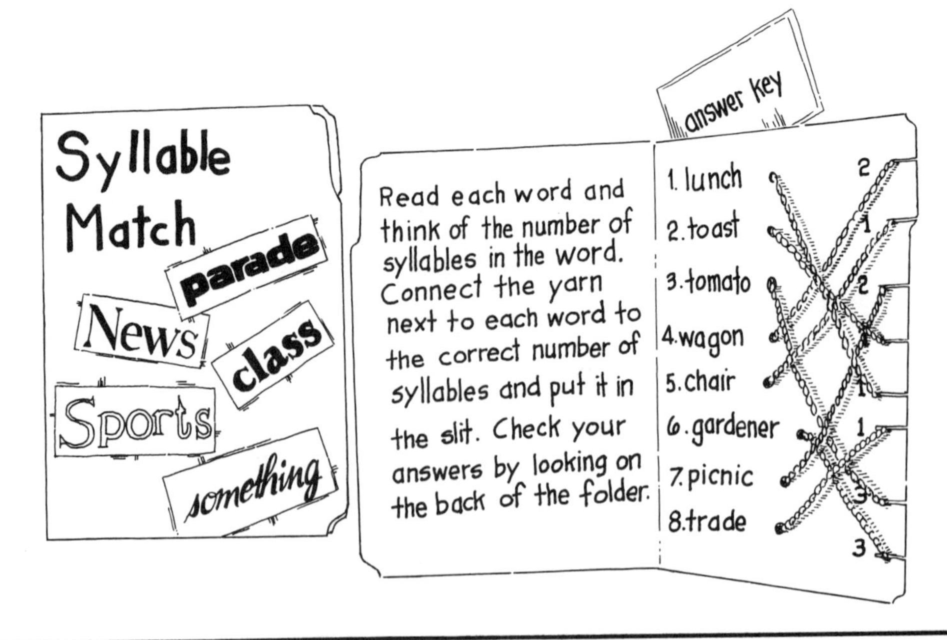

MATERIALS: File folder, newspapers and/or magazines, yarn.

CONSTRUCTION OF FOLDER: Based on the learner's vocabulary, decorate the front of the folder with words cut from newspapers or magazines.

Inside, list eight to ten words on the left-hand side of the folder and number each word. On the right-hand side of the folder, write the number of syllables in each word in random order.

Sample words include:

One Syllable		*Two Syllable*		*Three Syllable*	
lunch	toast	wagon	hurry	tomato	gardener
please	chain	photo	picnic	studio	checkerboard

Next to each word attach a piece of yarn and next to each number cut a ½″ slit in the right-hand edge of the folder.

On the back of the folder, next to each slit, write the answers.

DIRECTIONS ON FOLDER: Read each word inside the folder and think of the number of syllables in the word. Connect the yarn next to each word with the correct number of syllables and put it in the slit. Check your answers by looking on the back of the folder.

ADDITIONAL ACTIVITIES: Write the newspaper words listed on the cover of the folder on a piece of paper.

Write the number of syllables for each.

Use a newspaper to locate other words and determine the number of syllables.

Write ten words for objects found in the home and school and write the number of syllables for each.

Organize a *Scavenger Hunt* within the school or home. Have the learner find ten to fifteen objects and identify the number of syllables for each.

CHOW TIME

SKILL: Rhyming Words

PURPOSE: The learner will be able to match beginning consonants to the ending of a word and form new words that rhyme.

Note: Words that rhyme sound the same in their ending sounds.

MATERIALS: File folder, construction paper, magazines, cat food label, clear self-adhesive paper, grease pencil.

CONSTRUCTION OF FOLDER: On the cover of the folder, paste a cat food label.

Inside, cut and paste two bowls and a measuring cup. Add construction-paper spoons and paste them in the bowls. Obtain pictures of cats from magazines and paste them around the bowls and measuring cup. Cover the folder with clear self-adhesive paper or laminate. Using a grease pencil, write various beginning consonants (*b, m, h, p, r, v, c, f, s*) on the first bowl and on the other bowl write the ending sound *-at.* Write the directions for the folder on the measuring cup.

Write answers on the back of the folder.

DIRECTIONS ON FOLDER: Match the letters in the first bowl with the *-at* ending in the other bowl to form new words. How many can you make? Can you think of others?

Check your answers on the back after you have written the words on paper. Choose five words and write a sentence for each.

ADDITIONAL ACTIVITIES: Read several poems and find the rhyming words in the poems.

Write a poem and use rhyming words.

Reuse the folder by wiping off the beginning consonants and ending sound and writing others.

Sample beginning consonants and ending sounds include:

-it	*-ar*	*-ot*	*-in*	*-en*
bit	star	not	win	then
fit	bar	cot	pin	den
hit	car	dot	fin	hen
sit	far	hot	tin	pen

MIX AND MATCH: FILL THE CRACKS

SKILL: Vowel Sounds—Long and Short

PURPOSE: To be able to identify a long or short vowel sound in a word.

Note: A vowel is usually short if a word or syllable has one vowel at the

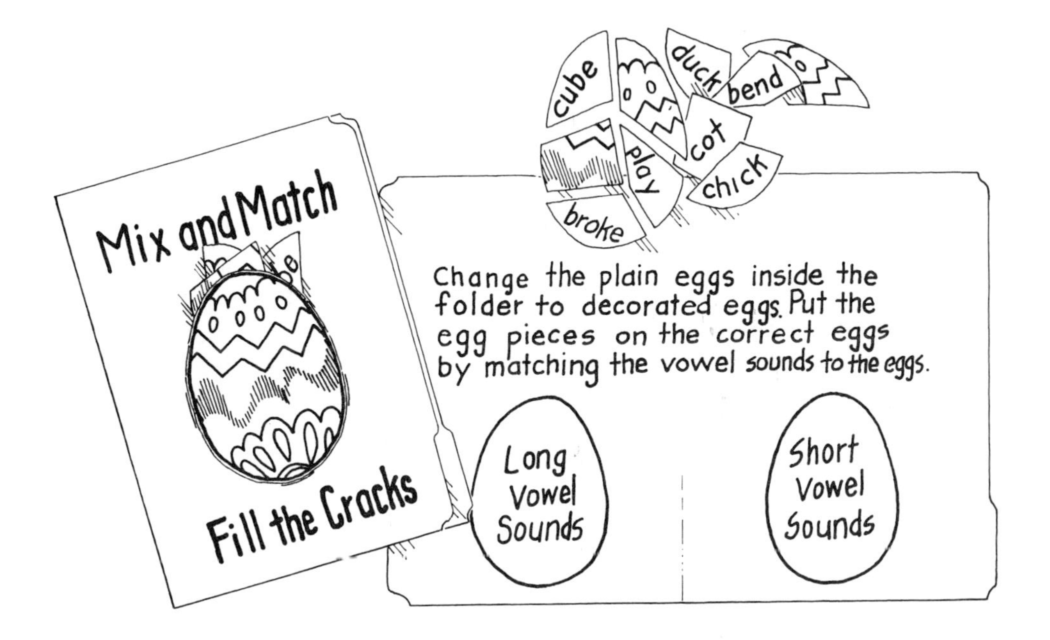

beginning or between two consonants. If a word has two vowels, the first vowel is usually long and the second one is silent.

MATERIALS: File folder, construction paper.

CONSTRUCTION OF FOLDER: Inside the folder, draw two large undecorated eggs. Write the words, *Long Vowel Sounds* on one egg and *Short Vowel Sounds* on the other.

From construction paper cut two eggs the same size as those inside the folder and decorate them. Cut each egg into five or six puzzle-like pieces. On the pieces for one egg write words containing long vowel sounds and on the other egg write words containing short vowel sounds.

Sample words include:

Long		*Short*	
light	bake	chick	bend
cube	teach	sink	cot
play	broke	duck	land

On the cover, paste a construction-paper egg, leaving the top open to use as a pocket to store the egg pieces.

DIRECTIONS ON FOLDER: Change the plain eggs inside the folder to decorated eggs. Put the egg pieces on the correct eggs by matching the vowel sounds to the eggs.

ADDITIONAL ACTIVITIES: Use two empty egg cartons and label one *Long Vowel Sounds* and the other *Short Vowel Sounds.* Cut out twenty-four small paper eggs and on twelve of them, write words that contain long vowels; on the others, write words that contain short vowels. Have the learner put the eggs in the correct carton.

Prepare an "egg hunt" by hiding the paper eggs in various locations in the classroom or home. Have the learner find the eggs and identify the vowel sound in each.

RIDE THE CLOUDS

SKILL: Vowel Sounds—Short

PURPOSE: Given one-syllable incomplete words, the learner will be able to put in the correct vowel to make a short-vowel-sound word.

Note: A vowel is usually short if a word or syllable has one vowel either at the beginning or between two consonants.

MATERIALS: File folder, construction paper, string-tie envelope.

CONSTRUCTION OF FOLDER: On the cover, draw a genie on a magic carpet flying through a cloud.

Inside, glue ten to twelve fluffy-looking white clouds. On each cloud write a word without the vowel.

Sample incomplete words include:

t_p	r_d	p_n	c_t
c_p	b_g	l_d	f_n
p_t	b_t	d_g	h_t

Make cloud-shaped worksheets from construction paper and store them in a string-tie envelope attached to the back of the folder.

Directions on Folder: Look at the clouds on the folder and make as many words as you can by adding vowels to each incomplete word. Take a cloud-shaped worksheet from the envelope and write each new word.

Additional Activities: Cut several large cloud shapes into three puzzle pieces each. On the beginning and end puzzle pieces, write a consonant. On the middle piece write a vowel. Have the learner put the pieces together to form words.

DIGGING UP BONES

Skill: Consonant Sounds—Hard and Soft *c*

Purpose: To be able to recognize the hard and soft *c* sounds in words.

Note: When the letter *c* is followed by *e, i,* or *y,* it usually has a soft sound similar to the *s* sound. When *c* is not followed by *e, i,* or *y,* it usually has a hard sound similar to the *k* sound.

Materials: File folder, construction paper, string-tie envelope.

Construction of Folder: Draw a doghouse and dog on the cover of the folder.

From construction paper draw and cut out two dog dishes and paste them inside the folder, leaving the top of each open to form a pocket. Label one dish *hard c* and the other dish *soft c.*

Make a set of approximately eighteen dog bones and on each bone write a word from the learner's vocabulary that contains either a *hard c* or a *soft c* sound.

Sample words include:

	Hard c			*Soft c*	
cage	music	bacon	center	face	juicy
candy	corner	traffic	police	fancy	decide
second	picnic	cube	prince	piece	celery

Make a large paper bone to use as an answer key and store word bones and answer key in a string-tie envelope attached to the back of the folder.

DIRECTIONS ON FOLDER: Read the words on the bones and place them in the correct dog dish. Check your work with the answer bone when you have finished.

ADDITIONAL ACTIVITIES: Write a sentence for ten of the *hard c* and *soft c* words on the bones.

Arrange the bones in alphabetical order.

Read a newspaper article and circle the *soft c* words in the article in red and the *hard c* words in blue.

Make additional bones and write words with *hard g* and *soft g*.

PLAYFUL KITTEN

SKILL: Reading Comprehension—Story Sequence

PURPOSE: The learner will be able to arrange sentences in sequence to form a story.

MATERIALS: File folder, poster board (9″ × 12″), photographs and/or magazine pictures, string-tie envelope.

CONSTRUCTION OF FOLDER: Decorate the front of the folder with a kitten playing with yarn.

Obtain several photographs or drawings of a kitten playing with yarn, which when put together will tell a story. On the back of each write a sentence about the picture.

Inside the folder draw several picture frames to fit the dimensions of the photographs or drawings.

For an answer key, write the sentences in order on a piece of poster board.

Store pictures and answer card in a string-tie envelope attached to the back of the folder.

DIRECTIONS ON FOLDER: The playful kitten has gotten into some mischief. Take the pictures out of the envelope and put them in the frames so that they tell a story. Read the story to yourself.

ADDITIONAL ACTIVITIES: Make a mobile. Write the sentences found on the back of the pictures on cards and attach them in sequence to a coat hanger.

Create and write a story about a pet that has gotten into mischief. (Suggested beginning: Has a pet of yours ever gotten into mischief?)

CANDLE COUNT

SKILL: Numeration—Number Recognition

PURPOSE: To be able to match numerals with sets of objects.

MATERIALS: File folder, construction paper.

CONSTRUCTION OF FOLDER: From construction paper cut out a large party cake and glue it on the cover, leaving the top open to serve as a pocket.

Inside, draw or paste several cutout cakes and on each write a number (from *1* to *9*) in random order.

Make candles, enough for the numbers on the cakes, and store them in the cake pocket on the front of the folder.

DIRECTIONS ON FOLDER: Take the candles out of the cake on the front of the folder. Open the folder and put the correct number of candles on each cake.

ADDITIONAL ACTIVITIES: Draw other cakes for classmates and family members and depending upon age, draw in the appropriate number of candles.

WHAT FLOOR, PLEASE?

SKILL: Numeration—Numerical Order

PURPOSE: The learner will be able to show numerals that use order.

MATERIALS: File folder, poster board (9″ × 12″), clear self-adhesive paper, grease pencil.

CONSTRUCTION OF FOLDER: On the cover of the folder, draw one or more skyscrapers.

Inside the folder, on the right half draw another skyscraper with many floors and windows. Next to the skyscraper, construct a slide device by cutting a 2″-slit near the top and bottom of the building. Cut a strip, 1½″ × 12″, from poster board and divide it into sections. Label each section *first, second, third,* and so on in random order. This slide device will represent an outside elevator. The windows on the skyscraper next to the elevator should be numbered *1, 2, 3,* and so on.

On the other side of the folder, make a pocket. Use it to store task cards for the activity.

Sample tasks include:

- Slide the elevator up and down to match the number with the word.
- You deliver newspapers and you have to deliver the paper to the third floor. Put an X on the third floor.
- You have a package to deliver to the fifth floor. Put a circle on the fifth floor.

Cover the folder with clear self-adhesive paper so that the learner can write on the folder with a grease pencil.

DIRECTIONS ON FOLDER: Take an elevator ride by following the directions on the cards that are found in the elevator.

ADDITIONAL ACTIVITIES: Draw a picture of a skyscraper or other large building and number the floors using words and numerals.

Cut out building shapes that represent stores or houses on a familiar street. Have the learner order them first, second, third, and so on.

Take the learner on an elevator ride. Stop at the different floors.

POT OF GOLD

SKILL: Division—Facts for *2* and *3*

PURPOSE: Given the division facts for *2* and *3,* the learner will know the quotient.

Note: The *quotient* is the answer in division.

MATERIALS: File folder, construction paper.

CONSTRUCTION OF FOLDER: Make two black kettles from construction paper and paste one on each side of the inside of the folder. Paste all sides of the kettles except the top so that there is an opening. On one kettle write the number *2* and on the other write the number *3.*

On the front cover, make a kettle pocket to store half-dollar-sized gold paper coins. On each coin write a division fact whose quotient is *2* or *3.*

Cut a large shamrock and write down all the facts with the answers. Store it in the front pocket.

Decorate the rest of the folder with shamrocks.

DIRECTIONS ON FOLDER: Take the gold coins out of the kettle on the cover. Look at the fact and place each coin within the kettle inside the folder that corresponds with the correct answer. Check your coins with the answer key shamrock when you have finished.

ADDITIONAL ACTIVITIES: On a large paper shamrock, write several division facts that have quotients of *2* and *3.*

This same folder can be made using other division facts and quotients.

Use an old kitchen pot or kettle to store cutout paper coins with division facts written on them. The learner can then choose several coins to solve each day.

ALL ABOARD

SKILL: Division—Facts for *3* and *4*

PURPOSE: Given the division facts for *3* and *4,* the learner will know the quotient.

Note: The *quotient* is the answer in division.

MATERIALS: File folder, construction paper, magazine pictures, string-tie envelope.

CONSTRUCTION OF FOLDER: Cut a train from construction paper or use a magazine picture depicting a train with cars. Paste it around the outside of the folder.

Inside, draw another train and include two baggage cars, leaving the top of the baggage cars open to form pockets. Write the number *3* on one car and the number *4* on the other.

Make twenty suitcases from construction paper and write a division fact on each whose quotient is *3* or *4.* Also, make one large suitcase with facts and answers to use as an answer key.

Store the suitcases in a string-tie envelope attached to the back of the folder.

DIRECTIONS ON FOLDER: Take the suitcases out of the envelope. Look at the fact on each suitcase and then place it in the baggage car with the correct answer. Check your answers with the large suitcase answer key when you have finished the activity.

ADDITIONAL ACTIVITIES: Use the paper suitcases as drill cards.

From cigar boxes make two suitcases. Label one *3* and the other *4.* Have the learner put the suitcases from the folder activity in the correct suitcase (box).

LOOKING GOOD

SKILL: Division—Facts for *5* and *6*

PURPOSE: Given the division facts for *5* and *6,* the learner will know the quotient.

Note: The *quotient* is the answer in division.

MATERIALS: File folder, aluminum foil, construction paper, clear self-adhesive paper, string-tie envelope.

CONSTRUCTION OF FOLDER: On the cover of the folder, glue a mirror made from foil or silver paper.

Inside, glue the top half of a large construction-paper comb without teeth. Spaced evenly on the comb, write division facts whose quotients are *5* or *6*.

From construction paper make a set of teeth and on each write the number *5* or *6*.

Cover the folder with clear self-adhesive paper and then slit the edge of the comb so the teeth will fit in.

Put the teeth into a string-tie envelope attached to the back of the folder.

DIRECTIONS ON FOLDER: You're looking good if you can match the division facts to their answers by slipping the teeth of the comb into the comb.

ADDITIONAL ACTIVITIES: Make other folders, similar to this, using different facts and answers.

PICK A POCKET

SKILL: Subtraction with Renaming (Borrowing)

PURPOSE: Given subtraction examples, the learner will be able to subtract hundreds, tens, and ones using renaming.

MATERIALS: File folder, scraps of cloth, construction paper, clear self-adhesive paper, grease pencil.

CONSTRUCTION OF FOLDER: To decorate the cover of the folder, cut out and glue a cloth or paper pocket.

Inside the folder, glue six to eight paper pockets that have a flap that lifts up. On the outside of the flap, write subtraction examples.

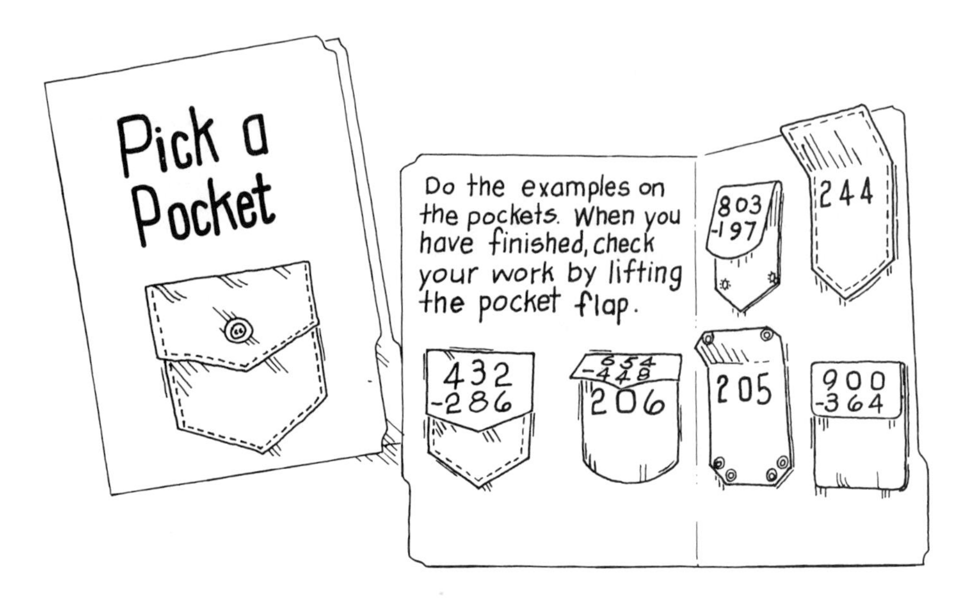

Sample examples include:

432	654	927	724	816	582
−286	−368	−538	−195	−437	−384

Under the flap write the answers to the examples.

Cover the folder with clear self-adhesive paper and have the learner write the answers with a grease pencil.

DIRECTIONS ON FOLDER: Do the examples on the pockets. When you have finished, check your work by lifting the flap on the pockets.

ADDITIONAL ACTIVITIES: Think of several three-digit numbers. Write and solve subtraction examples using these numbers.

Prepare small manila envelopes that include several subtraction examples or subtraction word problems within each. Have the learner "pick a pocket" to complete each day.

HELP TIPPY FIND THE TIME

SKILL: Telling Time—Hour

PURPOSE: The learner will be able to tell time to the hour.

MATERIALS: File folder, poster board (9″ × 12″).

CONSTRUCTION OF FOLDER: On the cover, draw a small mouse and a large clock with a pendulum.

Draw another large clock with a pendulum on the right side within the folder. Then construct two slide devices by making a 2″-slit on the top and bottom of the clock face section and two more slits opposite these beside the clock.

Use poster board to make two strips about 1½″ × 12″ that will fit into the slits on the folder. Divide each strip into an equal number of sections. On one strip write various times to the hour such as 1:00, 8:00, 12:00; on the other strip draw clock faces corresponding to these times. Number each clock face section on the strip and give a letter of the alphabet to each section on the time strip.

Draw a mouse (Tippy) and write the directions on the other side of the folder.

DIRECTIONS ON FOLDER: Help Tippy find the time by moving the slides up and down and matching the clock face to the written time. Take a piece of paper, number it, and write your answers by using the letters next to the time.

ADDITIONAL ACTIVITIES: Once the learner has become proficient in telling time to the hour, other strips can be made for the half-hour, quarter-hour, five minutes, or minute.

TEMPERATURE CONTROL

SKILL: Reading a Thermometer

PURPOSE: The learner will be able to read a thermometer.

MATERIALS: File folder, newspaper weather reports, red and white yarn or ribbon, posterboard (9″ × 12″).

CONSTRUCTION OF FOLDER: On the cover of the file folder, glue weather reports containing temperatures from the newspaper.

On the right side within the folder, draw a thermometer. Make a yarn or ribbon pulley to represent the mercury in the thermometer. To make the pully cut a slit on the top and bottom of the thermometer and pull the yarn or

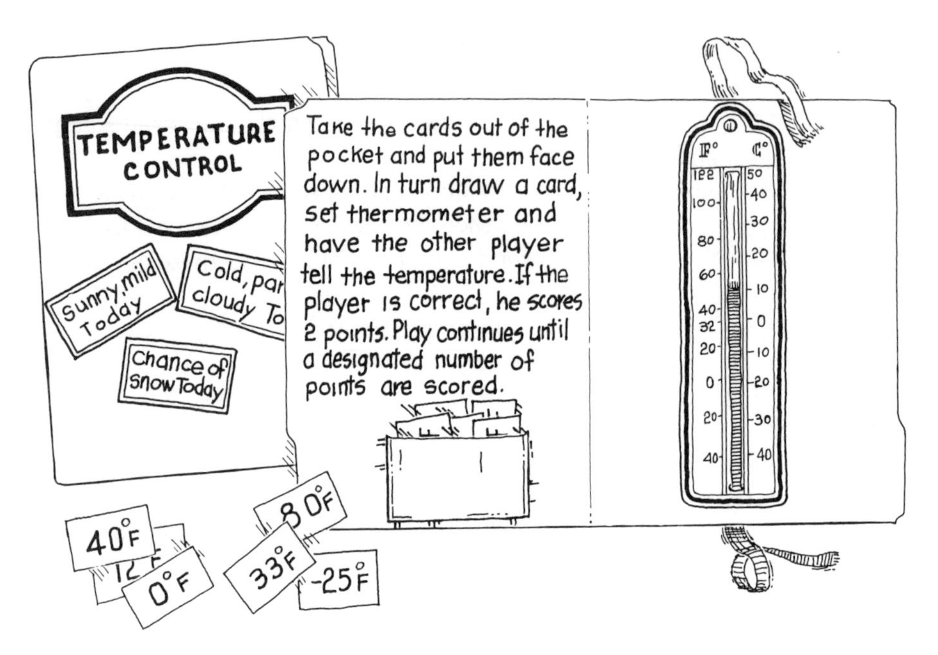

ribbon through and tie in the back. Use eight inches of each color (red and white) of yarn or ribbon and sew together.

Make several cards containing temperatures and store in a construction-paper pocket on the other side of the folder.

DIRECTIONS ON FOLDER: (two players) Take the cards out of the pocket and put them face down. In turn, draw a card, set the thermometer, and have the other player tell the temperature. If the player is correct, two points are scored. Play continues until a designated number of points are scored.

ADDITIONAL ACTIVITIES: Record temperatures in various rooms in school or home and compare the temperatures for several days.

Provide practice in reading a centigrade thermometer by using the thermometer on the folder and making a set of cards for Celsius degrees.

45 R.P.M.

SKILL: Fractions—Renaming

PURPOSE: Given a proper fraction, the learner will be able to rename it in lowest terms.

MATERIALS: File folder, construction paper.

CONSTRUCTION OF FOLDER: Inside the folder paste six to eight cutout records. On the record labels write fractions in lowest terms. (Examples: 1/4, 2/3, 3/4.)

Make other records that are the same size as those on the folder. On the labels of these records write fractional equivalents that when renamed will match those inside the folder. (Examples: 2/8, 4/6, 6/8.)

On the cover, paste a large construction-paper record leaving the top open to serve as a storage pocket for the records.

DIRECTIONS ON FOLDER: Take the records out of the cover pocket. Rename the fraction on each into lowest terms and match it with the record inside.

ADDITIONAL ACTIVITIES: Use the records to add or subtract fractional numbers with like and unlike denominators.

Make a set of "broken records" from construction paper. Cut each into selected fractional parts and have the learner put them together to make them whole.

GONE BANANAS

SKILL: Fractions—Equivalents

PURPOSE: Given a fractional part, the learner will be able to identify the fractional equivalent.

MATERIALS: File folder, magazine pictures, poster board (9″ × 12″), string-tie envelope.

CONSTRUCTION OF FOLDER: Inside the folder, draw a bunch of bananas and color parts of each banana to show a specific fractional part. Near the bananas write the caption, *Join the Bunch.*

Write fractions on cards corresponding to the fractional parts on the bananas. (Examples: 4/5, 1/2, 1/8, 1/3, 1/4.)

Store cards in a string-tie envelope attached to the back of the folder.

DIRECTIONS ON FOLDER: Join the bunch by placing each card on the banana that shows the fraction it represents.

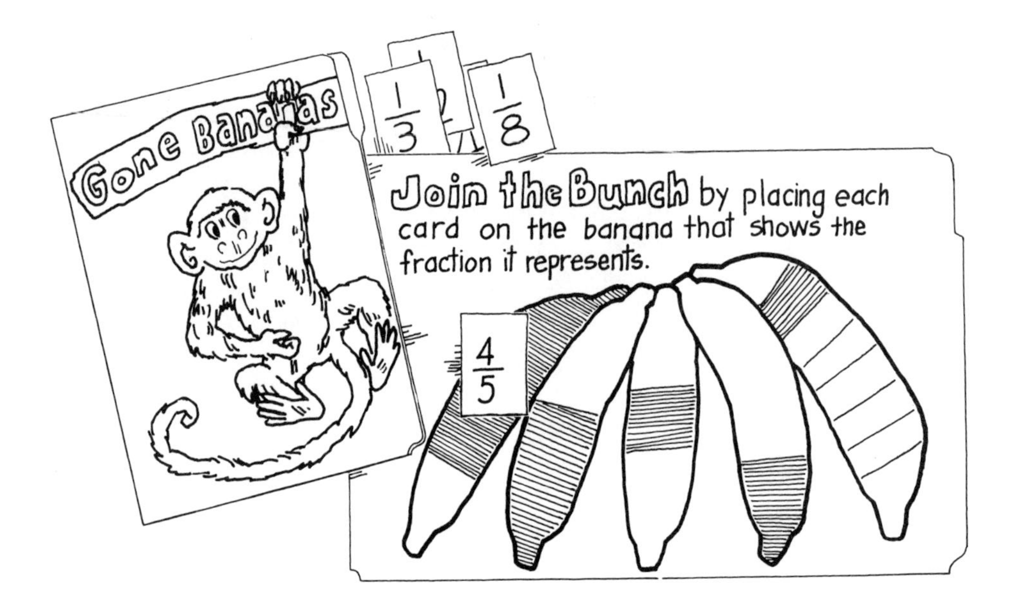

ADDITIONAL ACTIVITIES: Make a bunch of bananas. Use the fractional cards from the activity and color in, for each banana, the fractional part the cards represent.

Make "mixed up bananas" in which different construction-paper bananas are cut into various fractional parts and can be joined together to form a whole.

EGG HUNT

SKILL: Multipurpose

PURPOSE: The learner will be able to reinforce a particular skill depending upon need.

MATERIALS: File folder, egg stickers, greeting cards, construction paper, string-tie envelope.

CONSTRUCTION OF FOLDER: Inside the folder, make a game course by using egg stickers or egg-shaped cutouts. Designate a "start" by a rabbit cutout and a "finish" with a basket of eggs.

Decorate the inside and outside of the folder with spring greeting card pictures.

Game cards, in the shape of eggs, are designed for a particular skill.

A string-tie envelope is stapled on the back of the folder to store cards, markers, and die.

DIRECTIONS ON FOLDER: Help the rabbit find the basket of eggs. (Two players) Put cards face down. In turn, roll die, pick an egg card, give answer, and move the number of places on die if your answer is correct. The first player to reach the basket of eggs (finish) is the winner.

ADDITIONAL ACTIVITIES: Make cards to reinforce such skills as number or alphabet sequence, colors, geometric shapes, initial or final consonants, and uppercase and lowercase letters.

Design additional game boards on folders by using seasonal greeting cards and stickers.

DINO-WALK

SKILL: Multiplication—Facts for the *3* and *4* tables

PURPOSE: The learner will be able to recall the products for the *3* and *4* tables in multiplication.

Note: The *product* is the answer in multiplication.

MATERIALS: File folder, coding label dots, poster board (12″ × 18″), dinosaur coloring book or comic book, string-tie envelope.

CONSTRUCTION OF FOLDER: By using both sides of the inside of the folder draw a large outline of a dinosaur. Stick coding label dots (or dots you make from construction paper) around the outline of the dinosaur to form the game course.

Decorate the front of the folder with pictures of drawn or cutout dinosaurs.

Cut game cards 2″ × 6″ from poster board and divide into three equal sections. Write a multiplication fact in each section.

Attach an envelope to the back of the folder to store cards and markers.

DIRECTIONS ON FOLDER: (Two players) Take cards out of the envelope and put them face down. In turn, draw a card and give the answer for each fact on the card. If all three sections are answered correctly, move three spaces on the dinosaur; two answers correct, move two spaces; one answer correct, one space.

ADDITIONAL ACTIVITIES: Besides using a dinosaur, other large animals such as a lion, tiger, or elephant may be used.

SATURDAY MATINEE

SKILL: Multipurpose

PURPOSE: The learner will be able to reinforce a particular skill depending upon need.

MATERIALS: File folder, pictures from book, magazine and/or newspaper, poster board (9″ × 12″), string-tie envelope, die.

CONSTRUCTION OF FOLDER: Select a popular movie that several children have seen as the theme for the folder.

Obtain pictures from a newspaper or magazine advertisement of the movie or purchase an inexpensive children's book on the movie and use the pictures from the book. Paste the pictures on the cover and inside of the folder to decorate.

Inside, draw a game course and on selected places write penalty and fast forward moves. (Examples: Move ahead two spaces; lose one turn.)

Make a set of 2″ × 3″ cards from poster board to reinforce a particular skill.

Attach a string-tie envelope to the back of the folder to store game cards and playing pieces.

DIRECTIONS ON FOLDER: (Two players) Put cards face down. In turn, draw a card, give answer, and if answer is correct, roll die and move that number of places on game course. The first player to reach finish is the winner.

ADDITIONAL ACTIVITIES: Make cards to reinforce such skills as number facts, money, measurement, time, digraphs, or blends.

The title of the children's movie can be used as the title of the folder.

Other file folder games can be based on the theme of popular children's books.

CREATURES IN THE SEA

SKILL: Alphabetizing

PURPOSE: Given a selected group of words, the learner will be able to write them in alphabetical order according to their first and second letters.

Note: When putting words in alphabetical order, look at the first letter of each word and arrange them according to the sequence of the alphabet. If words have the same first letter, look at the second letter and place them alphabetically according to the second letter.

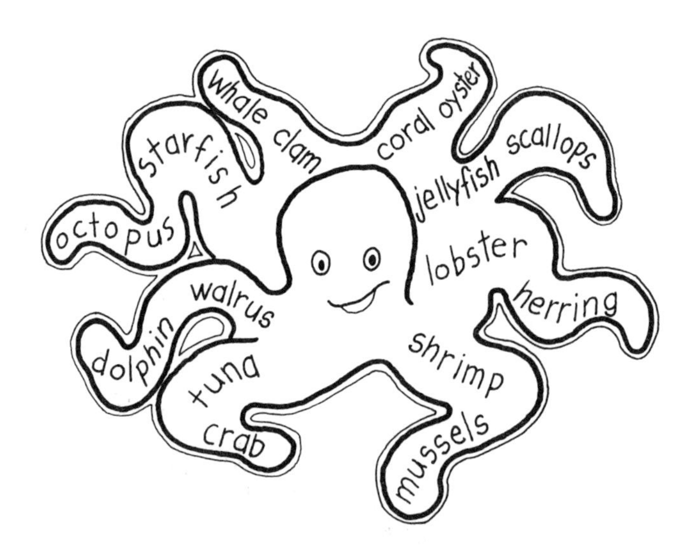

MATERIALS: Poster board (12″ × 18″).

CONSTRUCTION OF TASK CARD: Cut a large octopus from poster board. On each arm of the octopus write two words having to do with the sea.

Sample words include:

clam	herring	octopus	starfish
coral	jellyfish	oyster	tuna
crab	lobster	scallops	walrus
dolphin	mussels	shrimp	whale

DIRECTIONS ON TASK CARD: Take a piece of paper and write the words on the octopus's arms in alphabetical order.

ADDITIONAL ACTIVITIES: Use reference books such as an encyclopedia or dictionary to find information about the sea creatures and then draw an underwater scene and include as many of the creatures as possible.

Make other object task cards using shapes such as a car, fish, bird, or star and write words associated with the object.

ABC CAT

SKILL: Alphabetizing

PURPOSE: Given a selected group of words, the learner will be able to write them in alphabetical order according to their first and second letters.

Note: When putting words in alphabetical order, look at the first letter of each word and arrange them according to the sequence of the alphabet. If words have the same first letter, look at the second letter and place them alphabetically according to the second letter.

MATERIALS: Poster board (12″ × 18″ and 9″ × 12″), wallpaper scraps or felt remnants, magazine picture.

CONSTRUCTION OF TASK CARD: Draw and cut out a picture of a sleeping cat from the small poster board or use a magazine picture. From wallpaper scraps or felt remnants cut out an oval rug. Glue the cat to the rug. Then glue it to the large sheet of poster board. On the poster board write words to put in alphabetical order.

Sample words include:

bird	eat	milk	scratch
cat	hungry	mouse	sleep
chase	kitten	purr	watchful

Directions on Task Card: Write the words written around the cat in alphabetical order.

Additional Activities: Draw and cut out approximately twelve small cats from construction paper. Give each a name and write it on the cat's collar. Have the learner arrange them in alphabetical order.

LAY THEM STRAIGHT

Skill: Alphabetizing

Purpose: Given a selected group of words, the learner will be able to write them in alphabetical order according to their first and second letters.

Note: When putting words in alphabetical order, look at the first letter of each word and arrange them according to the sequence of the alphabet. If words have the same first letter, look at the second letter and place them alphabetically according to the second letter.

Materials: Poster board (12″ × 18″), construction paper.

Construction of Task Card: From construction paper cut out a bird's nest and paste it on the poster board leaving the top open to form a pocket. Draw a bird flying to the nest.

Cut out twelve small eggs from construction paper and on each write a name of a bird.

Sample bird names include:

blackbird	cardinal	mockingbird	pigeon
blue jay	chickadee	oriole	robin
canary	crow	parakeet	sparrow

Store the eggs in the nest pocket.

Make additional large eggs for the learner to use for the completion of the task.

DIRECTIONS ON TASK CARD: Take the eggs out of the nest and then write the names of the birds in alphabetical order on a large egg.

ADDITIONAL ACTIVITIES: Think of foods that birds eat and list them in alphabetical order.

Name places birds live and put these in alphabetical order.

Choose an egg from the nest and think of ten words that begin with the first letter in the word. Put these words in alphabetical order.

PARTY PLATE TASK CARD

SKILL: Alphabetizing

PURPOSE: The learner will be able to identify items and arrange them in alphabetical order.

Note: When putting words in alphabetical order, look at the first letter of each word and arrange them according to the sequence of the alphabet. If words have the same first letter, look at the second letter and place them alphabetically according to the second letter.

MATERIALS: Party paper plate, self-adhesive paper, grease pencil.

CONSTRUCTION OF TASK CARD: Use a party or birthday paper plate for this task card and on the back of the plate write tasks that correspond with the pictures on the plate.

Sample tasks include:

- Find ten objects on the plate and write the names of the objects in alphabetical order.
- Write the names of the colors found on the plate in alphabetical order.
- If you had a party, what would you have to eat? Write the names of the food in alphabetical order.

Cover the tasks on the plate with clear self-adhesive paper and circle the tasks you want the learner to complete with a grease pencil.

DIRECTIONS ON TASK CARD: Complete the task(s) that are circled.

ADDITIONAL ACTIVITIES: If you were going to have a party, who would you invite? Write the names of the children in alphabetical order.

Write a title for the task card based on the theme of the plate.

Collect and label party favors such as hats, balloons, napkins, toys, and horns for the learner to put in alphabetical order.

COMIC TASK

SKILL: Reading—Comprehension

PURPOSE: The learner will be able to complete a task after reading and comprehending a book.

MATERIALS: Comic books, index cards (3″ × 5″), paper clips.

CONSTRUCTION OF TASK CARD: Obtain comic books of interest to the learner and with a paper clip attach an index card to the cover of each. On each card write tasks for the specific comic book.

Sample tasks include:

- Make a puzzle of your favorite part of the story.
- Continue the adventure of the comic by making a small comic book of your own.
- Make a puppet of the most important character.
- List the main characters. Put them in alphabetical order.

DIRECTIONS ON TASK CARD: Read the comic book and complete the task(s).

ADDITIONAL ACTIVITIES: Invent a superhero of your own and design a comic book with your super-hero as the main character.

Use comics from the newspaper. Cut the frames apart. have the learner put the comic story back into sequence.

BOOKMARK TASK

SKILL: Reading—Comprehension

PURPOSE: The learner will be able to complete a task after reading and comprehending a book.

MATERIALS: Bookmark or poster board (2″ × 6″).

CONSTRUCTION OF TASK CARD: Make a bookmark from poster board or obtain a free one from a library or bookstore. On the back of the bookmark write specific tasks for a book and place the bookmark in the book.

Sample tasks include:

- Make a puppet of your favorite character.
- Paint a picture depicting a scene from the beginning, middle, and end of the book.
- Write a newspaper review of the book.
- Draw a book poster.

DIRECTIONS ON TASK CARD: Use the bookmark to help you keep your place while reading the book and then choose one or more of the tasks on the back of the bookmark to complete.

ADDITIONAL ACTIVITIES: Construct, in a shoebox, a three-dimensional scene of your favorite part of a book.

Pretend you are an author of a book and prepare a short oral report about the book.

Design a bookmark and include the title, author, and a short annotation of the book.

SPACE WORLD

SKILL: Nouns

PURPOSE: Given a picture, the learner will be able to identify the nouns.

Note: A *noun* is a word that names a person, place, or thing.

MATERIALS: Poster board (9″ × 12″), magazine pictures.

CONSTRUCTION OF TASK CARD: Choose a picture of interest to the learner such as an outer space scene or one having to do with a specific area of study. Paste it on the front of the poster board.

On the back of the card write the directions.

DIRECTIONS ON TASK CARD: Look at the picture on the other side. Take a piece of paper and write down all the *noun* words you can find.

ADDITIONAL ACTIVITIES: After you have completed your list of words, divide a paper into thirds and list them according to their category—person, place, thing.

Use the same picture and write down all the *verb* words you see.

Make a noun collage. Use old magazines and cut out noun pictures to use within your "collage." (A *collage* is a random arrangement of pictures and/or words pasted together. It is usually based on one theme.)

ALL ABOUT DINOSAURS

SKILL: Using References

PURPOSE: By using reference sources, the learner will be able to gather information and write a report.

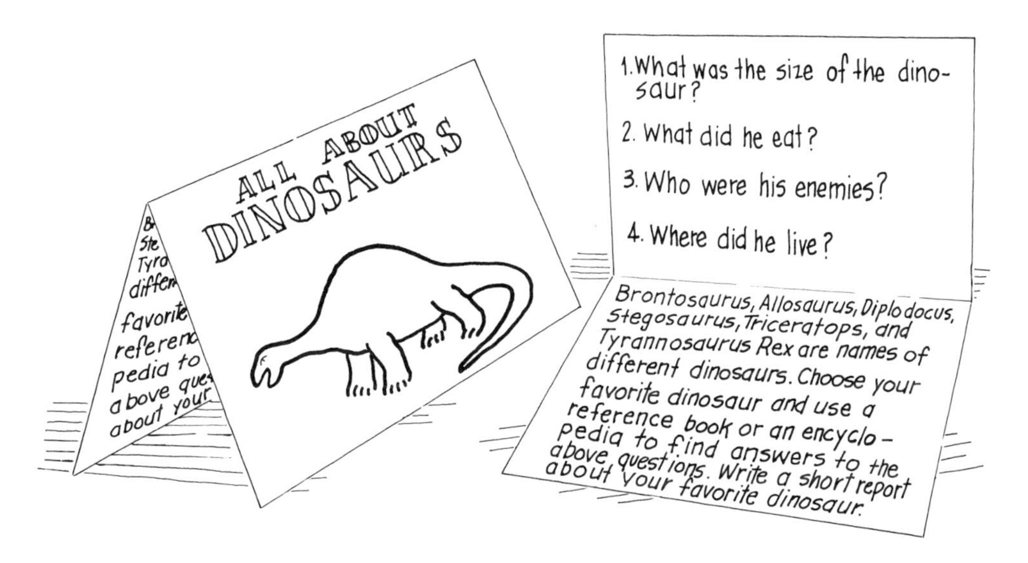

MATERIALS: Construction paper or poster board (9″ × 12″).

CONSTRUCTION OF TASK CARD: Fold the piece of construction paper or poster board in half. On the front, draw or paste a picture of a dinosaur.

Inside, on the top half of the folded task card, write general questions about dinosaurs.

Sample questions include:

- What was the size of the dinosaur?
- What did it eat?
- Where did it live?
- When did it live?
- What did it look like?
- Was it a meat eater or a plant eater?

On the bottom half, write the directions for using the card.

DIRECTIONS ON TASK CARD: *Brontosaurus, Allosaurus, Diplodocus, Stegosaurus, Triceratops,* and *Tyrannosaurus Rex* are names of different dinosaurs. Choose your favorite dinosaur and use one or several reference books to find the answers to the above questions. Write a short report about your favorite dinosaur.

ADDITIONAL ACTIVITIES: Draw or mount a picture of a dinosaur on poster board. Cut into several large pieces and have a friend put your puzzle together.

Make a dinosaur mobile by attaching small cutout dinosaurs to yarn and affixing them to a coat hanger.

Topics for other folded task cards include other animals or famous people.

A WILD THING TO DO

SKILL: Using References

PURPOSE: To be able to use reference materials to complete a creative project.

MATERIALS: Poster board (18″ × 24″), magazine pictures.

CONSTRUCTION OF TASK CARD: Decorate the poster board with wild animal pictures and then write tasks on the card.

DIRECTIONS ON TASK CARD: Think about your favorite wild animal. Go to the library and find information and pictures of the animal. Complete one of the following projects about the animal.

- Draw a pencil sketch.
- Write a report.
- Make a story book.
- Paint a picture.
- Make a mobile.
- Design a poster.

ADDITIONAL ACTIVITIES: Vary the theme of the task card by using different kinds of animal pictures—zoo, circus, pond, woodland, ocean.

Take the learner on a field trip to see the animals and explore their natural habitat.

Also, special television programs, movies, and filmstrips on the theme would enhance this activity.

MOBILE TASK CARD

SKILL: Using Reference Materials

PURPOSE: The learner will be able to gather information and write answers to questions about the state by using reference materials.

MATERIALS: Poster board (9″ × 12″), yarn.

CONSTRUCTION OF TASK CARD: Cut out a large shape of a state from poster board and attach it to a piece of yarn to form a mobile. On the back of the state write specific questions on that state for the learner to look up and answer using reference materials.

Sample questions include:

- What is the capital of the state?
- In what part of the United States is the state located?
- When was the state first settled?
- Who were the early settlers?

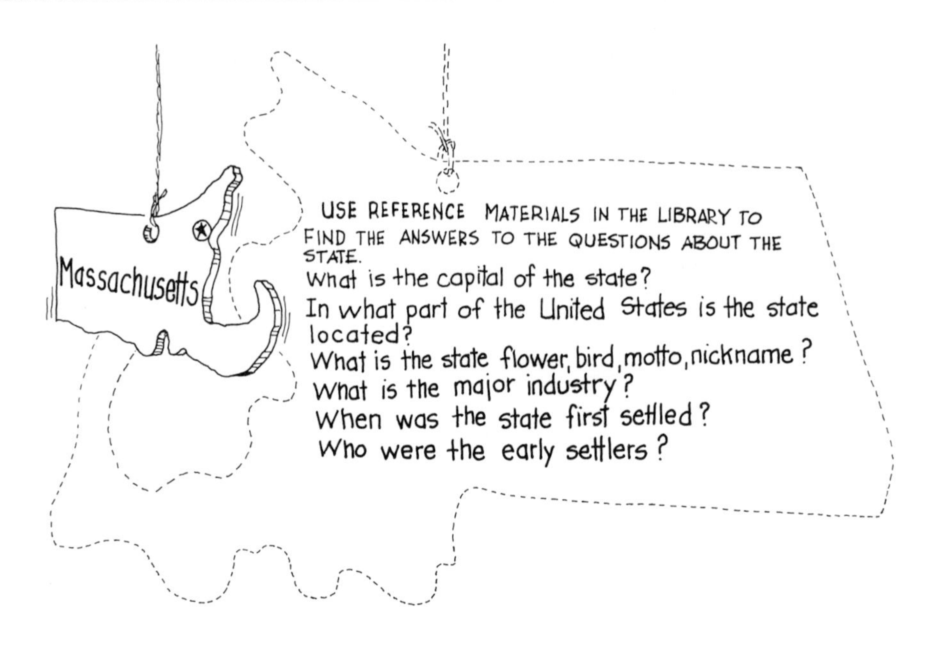

- What is the major industry?
- What is the state flower, bird, motto, nickname?

DIRECTIONS ON TASK CARD: Use reference materials in the library to find the answers to the questions about the state.

ADDITIONAL ACTIVITIES: Make mobiles using coat hangers and attaching several states by regions in the United States—northeast, southwest, midwest, and so on. Write questions on each state and let the learner choose a state of interest.

Instead of states, use countries, continents, or cities.

TRAVEL CARD

SKILL: Using References

PURPOSE: The learner will be able to gather information and write answers to questions about historical sites.

MATERIALS: Postcard, construction paper.

CONSTRUCTION OF TASK CARD: To make this task card, use a new or used postcard of a historical site. If the postcard is used, recycle it by covering the message side with construction paper. On the back of the postcard, write questions about the site.

Sample questions include:

- What is the name of the site?
- Where is it located?
- Why is it important?
- Would you like to visit it? Why?

DIRECTIONS ON TASK CARD: Use reference materials to find answers to the questions about the historical site.

ADDITIONAL ACTIVITIES: Instead of historical sites, use postcards of cities and states.

Choose a postcard of interest to the learner such as circus, transportation, or animals. On the back write tasks for the learner to do such as arithmetic examples or words to be divided into syllables.

STAND-UP CROSS-SHAPED TASK CARD

SKILL: Spelling

PURPOSE: By using selected spelling words, the learner will be able to complete the various tasks.

MATERIALS: Two pieces of poster board (8″ × 8″).

CONSTRUCTION OF TASK CARD: On each square of poster board, make a slit from the middle edge of one side to the center of the square. Put the squares together by joining them at the slits.

List the spelling words and write the directions for using the *Stand-Up Cross-Shaped Task Card* on one side. On the other sides, write tasks, each

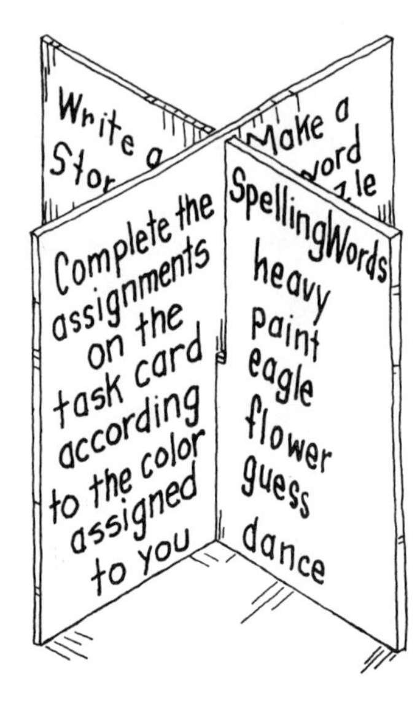

in a different color. Assign tasks on different days or to different learners depending upon the color.

Sample tasks include:

- Write the words in alphabetical order.
- Look up the words in the dictionary.
- Write a sentence for each word.
- Unscramble the letters in the words.
- Find the missing letters for the words.
- Make a "word search" using the words.
- Make a crossword puzzle for a friend.
- Write a story using the words.

DIRECTIONS ON TASK CARD: Complete the assignments on the task card according to the color assigned to you.

ADDITIONAL ACTIVITIES: Other *Stand-Up Cross-Shaped Task Cards* can be constructed for such academic areas as reading, language, mathematics, social studies, or science.

The title of the card varies with the skill.

Stand the task card on a table or desk and place along with it the supplementary materials to be used.

FUDGE DELIGHT

SKILL: Word Plurals—Ending in *y*

PURPOSE: Given selected words ending in *y*, the learner will write the plural forms.

Note: The *plural form* of a word means more than one. (When a word ends in *y* and has a consonant before it, usually the *y* is changed to *i* and *es* is added.)

MATERIAL: Poster board (9″ × 12″).

CONSTRUCTION OF TASK CARD: On poster board, draw and cut out a hot fudge sundae or a banana split. On the scoops of ice cream write words that end in *y* and can be made plural by changing the *y* to *i* and adding *es*.

Sample words include:

dry	candy	cry	cherry
baby	daisy	hobby	beauty
country	lady	strawberry	city

Write the directions on the back of the card.

DIRECTIONS ON TASK CARD: Make the words on the sundae mean more than one. Write the new words.

ADDITIONAL ACTIVITIES: Instead of words ending in *y*, use words ending in *ss*, *x*, *sh*, *ch*, *z*, or words ending in *f* or *fe*. Have the learner make these words plural.

HAPPY

SKILL: Creative Expression

PURPOSE: To be able to express one's feelings creatively through writing and pictures.

MATERIALS: Poster board (9″ × 12″), magazine pictures.

Make a list of things that make you happy. Choose one thing from your list and write a paragraph telling why it makes you happy.

CONSTRUCTION OF TASK CARD: On the front of the poster board, print in large letters the word *happy*. Decorate the task card with pictures that make people happy. On the back of the card write tasks.

Sample tasks include:

- Make a list of things that make you happy.
- Choose one thing from your list and write a paragraph telling why it makes you happy.
- Draw a picture of yourself doing something that makes you happy and explain.
- Cut pictures from a magazine of things that make you happy. Paste them on paper to make a collage.

DIRECTIONS ON TASK CARD: Read the tasks on the card and then choose one or more of the tasks to do.

ADDITIONAL ACTIVITIES: Take a survey of your friends or classmates. Find out and list the things that make them *happy*. Make a bar graph showing your findings. Note the similarities and differences.

Make other cards using words such as *big, little, quiet, soft, cold,* and *sad* and write tasks for these words.

ATTACH-A-TASK

SKILL: Creative Writing

PURPOSE: Given an object, the learner will be able to write a creative story using the object as the central theme of the story.

MATERIALS: Small object or toy, string or yarn, index card (3″ × 5″).

CONSTRUCTION OF TASK CARD: Choose an object such as a toy ship. With string or yarn attach an index card to the object. Write tasks on the card.
Sample tasks for the ship include:

- If this were an ocean liner, where would you like to travel? Write about your trip.
- You have been shipwrecked on an island. Write an imaginary log for the ten days you are there before you are finally rescued. Include what you did each day; what food you ate; what you saw; where you slept; and how you were rescued.

DIRECTIONS ON TASK CARD: Complete one or more of the tasks on the card.

ADDITIONAL ACTIVITIES: Other objects to use for this activity include:

toy airplane	basket	butterfly	feather
stuffed animal	balloon	baseball	bell

The title of this activity depends upon the object used.

COUNTDOWN

SKILL: Number Recognition—Counting to Ten

PURPOSE: To be able to count objects to ten and recognize the numbers and number words in random order.

MATERIALS: Poster board (9″ × 12″), primary workbook or print wrapping paper, construction paper, calendar.

CONSTRUCTION OF TASK CARD: Look in a primary workbook or on print wrapping paper for small pictures of objects that denote a certain number of things. For example, you might find one apple, two balloons, three flowers. Cut the objects out.

Divide the poster board into twelve 3″ × 3″ sections and paste a picture in each section, but not in numerical sequence.

Cut large number squares from an old calendar that represent the number of objects in the pictures. Write the word for the number on the back of each calendar square.

Make a construction-paper pocket to store the calendar squares and paste it on the back of the card. Write the directions for the activity on the pocket.

DIRECTIONS ON TASK CARD: Take the number cards out of the pocket. Count each set of objects and put the correct number card on it. Turn the number card over and read the word.

ADDITIONAL ACTIVITIES: Go on a *Scavenger Hunt* and find five buttons, three paper clips, four pencils, six pieces of paper.

Take an old calendar page and in each square write the word for the number.

NEWSY NUMBERS

SKILL: Number Recognition

PURPOSE: The learner will be able to recognize numbers within a newspaper.

MATERIALS: Poster board (6″ × 9″), newspaper, construction paper.

CONSTRUCTION OF TASK CARD: Cut items from newspapers that contain numbers (sports, index, date, temperature, advertisements) and glue onto poster board. Write the directions on the card.

DIRECTIONS ON TASK CARD: Look through a newspaper and find places where numbers are used. Make a collage of these numbers by cutting the sections out and pasting them on a sheet of construction paper. Read the numbers to a friend.

ADDITIONAL ACTIVITIES: Add *3* to each of the numbers.

Multiply each number by *2, 3,* and *4.*

Choose ten numbers and write the numbers that come before and after each.

ROLLING ALONG WITH MATH

SKILL: Addition—Facts to *15*

PURPOSE: To be able to compute basic addition facts to sums of *15.*

Note: The *sum* is the answer in addition.

MATERIALS: Poster board (9″ × 12″), magazine picture.

CONSTRUCTION OF TASK CARD: Draw a roller coaster or paste a picture of one on the poster board. In each car of the roller coaster write a number—*0* to *9*—in random order.

DIRECTIONS ON TASK CARD: Add *6* to each of the numbers on the roller coaster cars. Write each addition fact on paper.

ADDITIONAL ACTIVITIES: Add *7, 8,* and *9* to the numbers on the roller coaster cars.

Multiply the numbers on the cars by *4, 5,* and *6.*

BOX-A-TASK

SKILL: Addition and Subtraction—Computation

PURPOSE: The learner will be able to compute, by adding and substracting numbers with renaming, to the ones, tens, and hundreds.

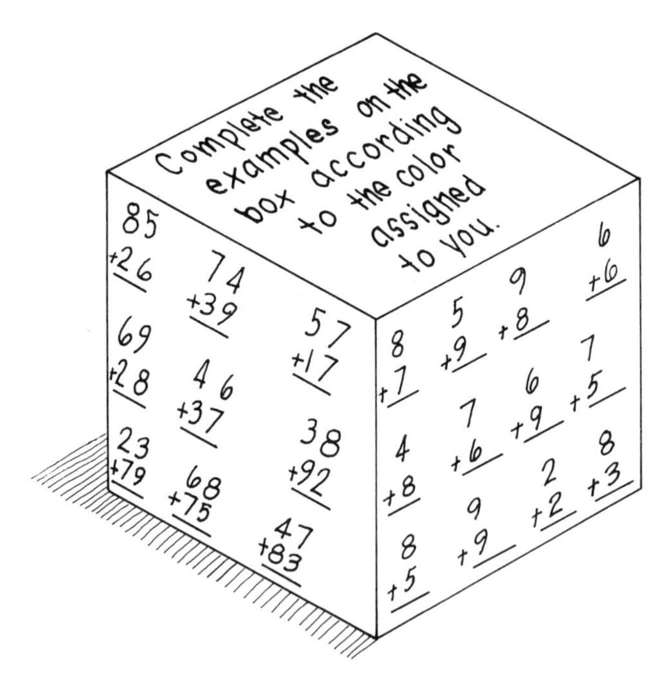

MATERIALS: Cardboard box, scrap wallpaper, plain or wrapping paper, index cards.

CONSTRUCTION OF TASK CARD: Cover a box of any size with plain paper, wrapping paper, or scrap wallpaper. Write a task on each of the six sides of the box or glue a card (size depends upon box) to each side. Code skill difficulty by writing addition and subtraction examples in a different color pen for each side.

Sample tasks for sides include:

- Blue pen—addition facts to sums of *18*
- Red pen—subtraction facts to *18*
- Green pen—addition examples of tens and ones with renaming
- Yellow pen—subtraction examples of tens and ones with renaming
- Purple pen—addition examples of hundreds, tens, and ones with renaming
- Orange pen—subtraction examples of hundreds, tens, and ones with renaming.

DIRECTIONS ON TASK CARD: Complete the examples on the side(s) of the box according to the color(s) assigned to you.

ADDITIONAL ACTIVITIES: This idea can easily be adapted to other skill areas.

SHOPPING SPREE

SKILL: Money—Word Problems—Addition and Subtraction

PURPOSE: Given selected grocery items, the learner will be able to solve word problems using addition and subtraction.

MATERIALS: Small paper bag, labels from food items or toy food items.

CONSTRUCTION OF TASK CARD: Begin with a small brown paper bag and use it as the task card. Gather labels from grocery items, or if available, obtain toy grocery items. Affix a price to the labels or items and put them inside the bag for use in solving the tasks.

On one side of the bag write money problems to correspond with the grocery items and on the other side write the title of the activity.

Sample word problems include:

- You are going to have a picnic. For the picinc you will need to buy a pound of hot dogs, hot dog rolls, potato chips, and six cans of soda. How much money will these items cost?

- If you give the cashier $10.00 for the items listed above, what will your change be?
- Add the prices of all the items in the bag. What is the total?
- Add the prices of the vegetable items in the bag. What is the total?
- What items could you buy for $5.00? List them.

DIRECTIONS ON TASK CARD: Use the items in the shopping bag to solve the problems written on the bag. Write your answers on paper.

ADDITIONAL ACTIVITIES: Set up a "mini-market" by using items such as empty milk and egg cartons, vegetable and fruit cans, cereal and cookie boxes, and coffee and orange juice cans. Price them and have the learner use these to solve money problems.

Have the learner role play a cashier in the "mini-market." Use toy money to make change.

Write money problems on sales tags for the learner to solve.

MENU TASKS

SKILL: Money—Word Problems—Addition and Subtraction

PURPOSE: By using a menu, the learner will be able to solve money word problems.

MATERIALS: Menu, index cards (3″ × 5″), paper clip.

CONSTRUCTION OF TASK CARD: Obtain a menu from an area restaurant. On several small cards, write word problems that pertain to the items on the menu. Attach the cards to the menu with a paper clip.

Sample tasks for cards include:

- You are going out to lunch and you have invited a friend. You have $4.00 to spend. What did you order and what was your total bill? How much change did you get back?
- For lunch you ordered a cheeseburger, an order of French Fries, a small root beer, and a chocolate ice cream cone. How much money did you spend?
- If you had $3.00, how many hot fudge sundaes could you buy? Would you have any change left over?

- For breakfast you ordered pancakes with sausages. How much did it cost?
- What is the most expensive item on the menu?
- What is the least expensive item on the menu?

DIRECTIONS ON TASK CARD: Use the menu to do the tasks on the cards.

ADDITIONAL ACTIVITIES: Instead of using a menu, use newspaper advertisement inserts or catalogs and write word problems associated with these.

STAND-UP TRIANGULAR TASK CARD

SKILL: Addition—Column with Tens and Ones

PURPOSE: To be able to compute the sum of three two-digit numbers with renaming.

Note: The *sum* is the answer in addition.

MATERIALS: Poster board (9″ × 12″).

CONSTRUCTION OF TASK CARD: Fold the poster board into fourths, lengthwise. Glue the two end sections together to form a base for a triangular-shaped figure. Write column addition examples near the base of each side of the figure. Under each example, on the base of the task card, write the answers for self-checking.

DIRECTIONS ON TASK CARD: Solve each column addition example on paper.

When you have finished check your answers by looking on the bottom of the task card underneath each example.

ADDITIONAL ACTIVITIES: This idea can easily be adapted to any math operation—addition, subtraction, multiplication, and division.

KEEP ON THE RIGHT TRACK IN MATH

SKILL: Multiplication—Facts, *2* table

PURPOSE: To be able to recall the *2* table in multiplication by writing the facts.

Note: The *product* is the answer in multiplication.

MATERIALS: Poster board (9″ × 12″), magazine pictures.

CONSTRUCTION OF TASK CARD: Paste a picture of a train or draw a train on poster board. Under the train draw a track and in between each tie of the track write a number—*0* to *9*—in random order.

DIRECTIONS ON TASK CARD: Multiply each number on the track by *2.* Copy each fact on paper.

ADDITIONAL ACTIVITIES: Multiply each of the numbers on the track by *3, 4,* and *5.*

Add *6, 7,* and *8* to each number on the track.

SPOUTING OFF FACTS

SKILL: Multiplication—Facts, *3, 4, 5* tables

PURPOSE: To be able to recall the *3, 4,* and *5* tables in multiplication by writing the facts.

Note: The *product* is the answer in multiplication.

MATERIALS: Poster board (9″ × 12″), construction paper.

CONSTRUCTION OF TASK CARD: Draw a whale or cut out and paste one onto poster board. Write the numbers *0* to *9* in random order on the whale. Decorate the task card with other sea life.

DIRECTIONS ON TASK CARD: Multiply each number on the whale by *3, 4,* and *5* and write each fact.

ADDITIONAL ACTIVITIES: This idea can easily be adapted to any math operation—addition, subtraction, multiplication, and division.

Also, different themes can be depicted depending upon learner interest. (Examples: circus, holidays, sports, historical sites)

POP-UP EGGS

SKILL: Multiplication—*2*- and *3*-Digit by *1*-Digit Numbers with Renaming

PURPOSE: Given selected example in multiplication, the learner will be able to multiply with renaming.

MATERIALS: Poster board (9″ × 12″), construction paper.

CONSTRUCTION OF TASK CARD: On poster board draw a basket with six to eight eggs in it. From construction paper cut egg shapes to fit over the eggs on the poster board. Glue the top edge of each cutout egg over the eggs on the poster board and write multiplication examples on the construction-paper eggs. Write the answers for the multiplication examples on the eggs on the poster board for self-checking.

DIRECTIONS ON TASK CARD: Solve each multiplication example on paper. Check your work when you are finished by "popping up" the eggs.

ADDITIONAL ACTIVITIES: Instead of using eggs, use peanuts in a dish or a house with windows and doors that open.

SNEAKER PACE

SKILL: Measurement—Inch, Foot

PURPOSE: To be able to measure objects to the nearest inch or foot.

MATERIALS: Poster board (12″ × 18″).

CONSTRUCTION OF TASK CARD: Draw and cut out a large outline of a sneaker from poster board. On the back of the sneaker write measurement tasks.

Sample tasks include:

- Measure from your chair to the teacher's desk.
- Measure from the door to the bookcase.
- Measure your sneaker or shoe.
- Measure your thumb.
- What is the difference between the length of your sneaker and your thumb?

DIRECTIONS ON TASK CARD: Use a 12-inch ruler and this sneaker card to complete the tasks.

ADDITIONAL ACTIVITIES: Measure to the nearest half-inch and quarter-inch.

Complete the activity using metrics.

Using a tape measure, measure your head, foot, waist, wrist, and height.

ICE SKATING SHAPE UP

SKILL: Perimeter of a Polygon

PURPOSE: The learner will be able to find the perimeter of a polygon.

Note: A *perimeter* is the distance around a closed figure. A *polygon* is a simple closed figure with sides. Examples of polygons are squares, rectangles, and octagons.

MATERIALS: Poster board (12″ × 18″).

CONSTRUCTION OF TASK CARD: Hold the poster board horizontally and in the center draw a large figure 8. Draw a pair of ice skates near the figure. Around the figure 8, draw six to ten geometric shapes and label the dimensions.

DIRECTIONS ON TASK CARD: The ice skaters have made many different patterns on the ice. Find the perimeter of each. Do your work on paper.

ADDITIONAL ACTIVITIES: Find the perimeter of objects around the classroom or home such as books, tables, and desks.

Measure your classroom, bedroom, or playroom and find the perimeter. Draw a floor plan of the room.

Cut geometric shapes from construction paper and have the learner measure the sides and find the perimeter.

BALLOONS FOR SALE

SKILL: Measurement—Inch

PURPOSE: To be able to measure to the nearest inch.

MATERIALS: Poster board (12″ × 18″), yarn, construction paper.

CONSTRUCTION OF TASK CARD: Cut six to eight balloon shapes from construction paper and glue onto poster board. Number each balloon. Use yarn of different lengths for the balloon strings.

DIRECTIONS ON TASK CARD: Measure each balloon string and write your answers on paper.

ADDITIONAL ACTIVITIES: Cut pieces of yarn, to represent worms, into various lengths. Put them in a small covered can. The learner will have fun measuring each "worm."

PLAYING CARD TASK

SKILL: Multipurpose

PURPOSE: Given a list of tasks, the learner will be able to reinforce a particular skill depending upon need.

MATERIALS: Playing card(s), paper clip, construction paper.

CONSTRUCTION OF TASK CARD: Choose a number playing card and cover the back of it with construction paper. Write tasks that correspond to the number on the card.

Sample tasks include:

- Write as many addition and subtraction examples as you can that will have this number as an answer. You should have at least ten.
- Add the numbers *6, 7, 8,* and *9* to this number and write the facts.
- Write the number that comes before and after this number.
- Write the word for this number.
- Draw a picture using this number.

Number each task and mark the ones you want to assign to the learner by inserting one or more paper clips on the task number.

DIRECTIONS ON TASK CARD: Use the playing card to do the task(s) that have been marked with the paper clip(s).

ADDITIONAL ACTIVITIES: Write and solve two addition and subtraction word problems using this number as an answer.

Find magazine pictures that show this number of things.

WORKSHEET TASK CARD

SKILL: Multipurpose

PURPOSE: The learner will be able to reinforce a particular skill depending upon need.

MATERIALS: Worksheets, poster board (9″ × 12″), clear self-adhesive paper, grease pencil.

CONSTRUCTION OF TASK CARD: Turn your favorite worksheets into permanent task cards by pasting the mimeographed copy onto poster board. Cover it with clear self-adhesive paper or laminate.

DIRECTIONS ON TASK CARD: Read the directions on the worksheet and write your answers with a grease pencil.

ADDITIONAL ACTIVITIES: Teacher-constructed worksheets can be made permanent for continual and long-lasting use.

Have the learner create a worksheet for a specific skill. Make it permanent for other learners to use.

THEME-A-TASK

SKILL: Multipurpose

PURPOSE: The learner will be able to reinforce a particular skill depending upon need.

MATERIALS: Poster board (9″ × 12″), magazine pictures, clear self-adhesive paper, grease pencil.

CONSTRUCTION OF TASK CARD: Find a magazine based on a theme and caption it. Around the picture and title write math facts, problems, or words, depending upon the skill to be reinforced.

Cover the card with clear self-adhesive paper or laminate.

Sample pictures and captions include:

Dinosaur pictures: *Math is Dynamite*
Someone on a bicycle: *Moving Ahead in Spelling*
Piggy bank and coins: *Save for a Rainy Day*
Picture of a bee: *Bee—Careful—Subtract*
Old schoolhouse with bell: *Math Time*
Hot air balloon: *Up, Up, and Away*

DIRECTIONS ON TASK CARD: Complete tasks on the card by using a grease pencil or by copying on paper.

ADDITIONAL ACTIVITIES: In place of magazine pictures, use the learner's drawings.

STAR PLAYERS

SKILL: Multipurpose

PURPOSE: The learner will be able to reinforce a particular skill depending upon need.

MATERIALS: Sports cards, poster board (6″ × 9″).

CONSTRUCTION OF TASK CARD: Use a baseball card, football card, or other card of interest and staple or fasten it to the poster board. Around the card write tasks depending upon the skill to be reinforced.

DIRECTIONS ON TASK CARD: Bat 100 by correctly completing the work on the task card.

or

Score a touchdown by correctly completing the work on the task card.

ADDITIONAL ACTIVITIES: Tasks for card can include words with long- and short-vowel sounds, hard and soft *g* and *c* words, or math facts.

The sports card, which is on the task card, can be given to the learner when the work is completed.

For permanent task cards, several sports cards can be glued on poster board and the tasks written around them.

In place of sports cards, holiday or novelty stickers can be used.

NAME TASK CARD

SKILL: Multipurpose

PURPOSE: By using the letters in the learner's first name, the learner will be able to complete tasks.

MATERIALS: Poster board (6″ × 9″), clear self-adhesive paper, grease pencil.

CONSTRUCTION OF TASK CARD: Have the learner write his or her first name in a decorative way on the poster board.

When the card is decorated, write individual tasks on it for the learner. Sample tasks include:

- Think of as many other names as you can that have the same beginning sound as yours and write them down.
- Use the letters in your name to write as many words as you can.
- What is the vowel sound in your name? Write ten words with that vowel sound.
- Can you divide your name in syllables? If you can, divide it.
- Write the letters that come before and after each letter in your name.

Cover the card with clear self-adhesive paper and circle the tasks you want the learner to complete with a grease pencil.

DIRECTIONS ON TASK CARD: Complete the circled task(s) on the back of your name card.

ADDITIONAL ACTIVITIES: Write an autobiography and include your hobbies, pets, favorite food, color, and anything else of interest to you. Title it your first name.

Instead of having the learner's first name on the card, write the learner's street, city, state, or month of birth.

ON THE MOVE WITH GAME BOARDS

BUSY B

SKILL: Consonant—*b*—Beginning, Medial, Final

PURPOSE: The learner will be able to recognize the position of the consonant *b* in a word.

MATERIALS: Poster board (18″ × 24″), magazine or workbook pictures, paper clip, paper brad.

CONSTRUCTION OF GAME BOARD: On poster board draw a large letter *B*. Use the outline of the *B* to form a game course. Evenly divide the course into spaces and mark *Start* and *Finish* in the center of a daisy-type flower. Draw a picture of a bee about every four to five spaces. In the other spaces paste pictures of words that have *B* in them. Find pictures in old magazines or workbooks.

Write the title of the game in the upper center portion of the letter *B*. In the lower center portion make a paper-clip spinner by inserting a paper brad through a paper clip and affixing it to the poster board. Write the directions on the back of the game board.

DIRECTIONS ON GAME BOARD: (two to four players) Place markers on *Start*. In turn, spin spinner, move that number of spaces on board, say the word for the picture and tell if *B* is in the beginning, middle, or end of the word. When a player lands on a bee, the player takes another turn. The first player to land on the flower (*Finish*) wins the game.

ADDITIONAL ACTIVITIES: Other letter game boards can be constructed.

(Examples: *C*—hard and soft *c* words; *G*—hard and soft *g* words; *M*—beginning, medial, final)

UP, UP, AND AWAY

SKILL: Contractions

PURPOSE: Given a selected contraction, the learner will be able to identify the two words it stands for.

Note: A *contraction* is a short way of writing two words. One or more letters are left out and an apostrophe is put in its place.

MATERIALS: Poster board (18″ × 24″ and 9″ × 12″), paper clip, paper brad.

CONSTRUCTION OF GAME BOARD: Draw a brightly colored hot air balloon on the poster board. In the upper portion of the balloon make a zig-zag game course. Mark *Start* and *Finish* on the course and also several reward and penalty moves.

Sample reward and penalty moves include:

Got caught in a windstorm. (Move ahead two spaces.)
What a beautiful sight! (Take another turn.)
The wind pulled you the wrong way. (Go back two spaces.)

Make game cards by using the other piece of poster board and writing a contraction on each.

Sample contractions include:

isn't	wouldn't	can't	you've
didn't	let's	there's	we've
they'll	I've	we're	that's
doesn't	who's	won't	wasn't

Provide a paper-clip spinner or affix one to the game board.

DIRECTIONS ON GAME BOARD: (two to four players) Place markers on *Start* and put cards face down. In turn, draw a card, say the two words that make up the contraction, spin the spinner, and move that number of places on the board if the answer is correct. If the answer is incorrect, the player does not move. Also, follow all other directions on the board. The first player to reach *Finish* is the winner.

ADDITIONAL ACTIVITIES: Make cards for abbreviations or compound words instead of contractions.

JOURNEY TO OUTER SPACE

SKILL: Antonyms

PURPOSE: Given a selected word, the learner will be able to give an antonym for the word.

Note: Antonyms are words that are opposite in meaning.

MATERIALS: Poster board (24″ × 36″ and 12″ × 18″), coding label dots, construction paper, magazine pictures and/or postcards, string-tie envelope.

CONSTRUCTION OF GAME BOARD: Paste space pictures, found in magazines or on postcards, across the top of the poster board. By using coding label dots make four evenly spaced vertical game courses. Draw stars on selected dots on each game course. Mark the bottom dot for each *Blastoff.*

Make a set of game cards from the 12″ × 18″ poster board and on each card write one antonym from each pair that follows.

Sample antonyms include:

slow—fast	sour—sweet	warm—cool	early—late
left—right	stop—go	open—close	rough—smooth
tiny—large	wide—narrow	begin—end	silent—noisy

In the corner of each card write the number *1, 2,* or *3.*

Cut four small rocket-shaped markers from different colors of construction paper.

Store cards and markers in a string-tie envelope attached to the back of the game board.

DIRECTIONS ON GAME BOARD: (two to four players) Choose a rocket and a game course and get ready to journey into outer space. Put the cards face down. In turn, draw a card, give an antonym for the word on the card, and move the number of spaces in the corner of the card. If you land on a star, take another turn. The first player to reach outer space (top of the game course) is the winner.

ADDITIONAL ACTIVITIES: In place of antonyms, make game cards for homonyms or synonyms.

FLUTTERBY

SKILL: Vocabulary Development—Pronunciation

PURPOSE: Given a selected list of words, the learner will be able to pronounce each.

MATERIALS: Poster board (24″ × 36″), clear self-adhesive paper, grease pencil.

CONSTRUCTION OF GAME BOARD: Cut a butterfly shape from the poster board. Around the edge of the butterfly draw a game course. Mark *Start* and *Finish* on the course. In several spaces write reward and penalty moves.

Sample moves include:

Spread your wings and fly. (Move ahead two spaces.)
Fly to the daisy. (Move ahead one space.)
Back to the cocoon. (Lose one turn.)

Cover the game with clear self-adhesive paper or laminate. With a grease pencil, write a word from the learner's vocabulary in the other spaces on the game course.

Provide markers and die to play the game.

DIRECTIONS ON GAME BOARD: (two to four players) In turn, roll die, move that number of places on the course, and say the word. If the word is mispronounced, go back to where you were. Follow all other directions written on the course. The first player to reach *Finish* is the winner.

ADDITIONAL ACTIVITIES: Give the definition of each word on the game course.

Use each word on the course in a sentence.

Instead of drawing a game course, if available, use butterfly or flower stickers.

HIPPO-HOP

SKILL: Alphabetical Order

PURPOSE: To be able to recognize the order of the letters of the alphabet.

MATERIALS: Poster board (24″ × 36″), coding label dots, paper clip, paper brad.

CONSTRUCTION OF GAME BOARD: Draw an outline of a hippopotamus on the poster board. Stick coding label dots or dots made from construction paper around the body of the hippopotamus. Mark *Start* and *Finish* on the course. On the other dots write a letter of the alphabet in random order.

Affix a paper-clip spinner to a corner of the game board.

DIRECTIONS ON GAME BOARD: (two players) Place markers on *Start.* In turn, spin spinner and move that number of places on board. Give the letter of the alphabet that comes after the one on the board. If answer is correct, stay there. If incorrect, move to where you were. The first player to reach *Finish* is the winner.

ADDITIONAL ACTIVITIES: Give the letter that comes before the letter on the board.

Think of a word that begins or ends with the letter on the board.

GET THE BEAT

SKILL: Syllabication

PURPOSE: Given a one- or two-syllable word, the learner will be able to tell how many syllables are in the word.

Note: A *syllable* is a word or part of a word that contains a vowel sound.

MATERIALS: Poster board (18″ × 24″, and 12″ × 18″), index card (3″ × 5″), paper clip, paper brad.

CONSTRUCTION OF GAME BOARD: On the poster board draw and cut out a drum. Make a spiral game course on the drum. Mark *Start* and *Finish.* Write reward and penalty moves in several spaces of the spiral course.

Sample moves include:

The crowd is pleased. (Take another turn.)
You've got the beat. (Take another turn.)
Dropped your sticks. (Go back one space.)

Make a set of cards in the shape of musical notes. On five cards draw a small musical note and on the others write words with one or two syllables.

Sample words include:

One Syllable		*Two Syllables*	
staff	march	banjo	trombone
play	drum	music	singer
horn	note	trumpet	organ
flute	clef	parade	guitar

Make a paper-clip spinner from the index card and provide markers.

DIRECTIONS ON GAME BOARD: (two players) Strike up the band by playing this game. Place markers on *Start* and put the cards face down. In turn, draw a card, tell the number of syllables in the word, spin, and move that number of spaces on the board if the answer is correct. If the answer is incorrect, player does not move. If a card with a musical note is drawn, player takes another turn. The first player to reach *Finish* is the winner.

ADDITIONAL ACTIVITIES: Have the skill be number recognition by making cards with numbers on them. Learner is to clap out the number on the card before moving on the game course.

Make a set of cards to give practice in recognizing musical symbols (quarter-note, eighth-note, G clef, and so on).

The game course can be drawn on a real toy drum.

DINOSAUR CHASE

SKILL: Addition and Subtraction—Facts to *18*

PURPOSE: To be able to recall the answers to the addition and subtraction facts to *18.*

Note: The *sum* is the answer in addition. The *difference* is the answer in subtraction.

MATERIALS: Two pieces of poster board (12″ × 18″), dinosaur picture.

CONSTRUCTION OF GAME BOARD: On one sheet of poster board glue or draw a picture of a dinosaur. Make a game course by drawing dinosaur footprints around the outline of the picture. On four to six selected footprints write *Trapped by dinosaur. Lose one turn.* Write *Start* and *Finish* on the course.

Cut game cards 2″ × 6″ from the other sheet of poster board and divide into three equal sections. Write an addition or subtraction fact in each section.

DIRECTIONS ON GAME BOARD: (two players) Put cards face down and markers on *Start.* In turn, draw a card and give answer for each section on the card. If all three sections are answered correctly, move three spaces; two answers correct, move two spaces; one answer, move one space. Follow all other directions written on the game. The first player to reach *Finish* is the winner.

ADDITIONAL ACTIVITIES: Cards can readily be changed for other skills. For example, provide spelling words to use in a sentence or small clocks for telling time.

CARD WHIZ

SKILL: Multiplication—Facts, *1–9* tables

PURPOSE: To be able to recall the products of the *1–9* multiplication tables.

Note: The *product* is the answer in multiplication.

MATERIALS: Poster board (24″ × 36″), deck of playing cards.

CONSTRUCTION OF GAME BOARD: Arrange playing cards around the poster board to form a game course. Mark *Start* and *Card Whiz* (*Finish*) on the game course.

Provide a die and markers for the game.

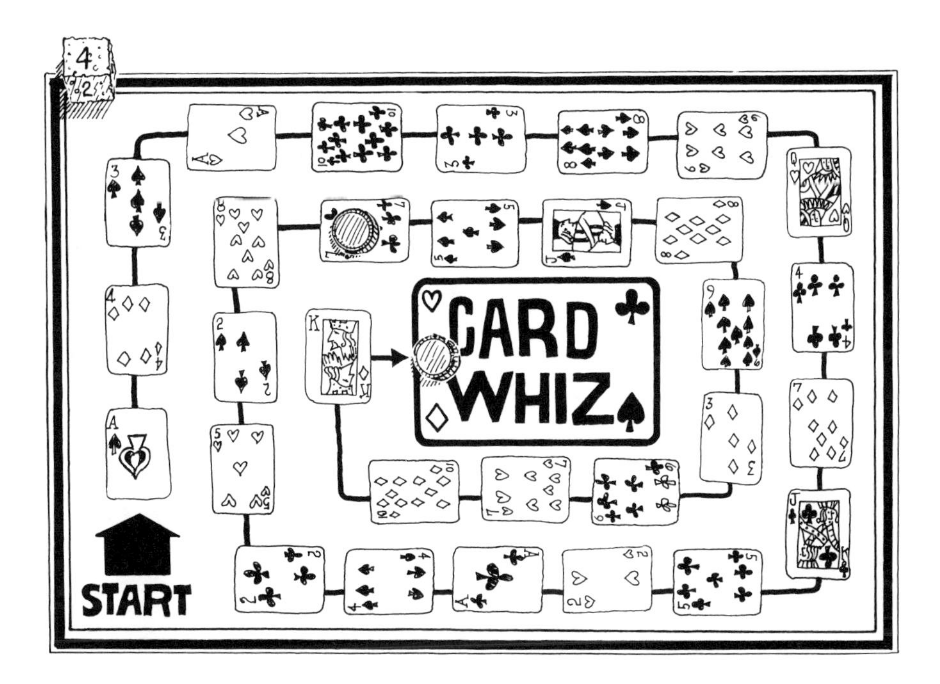

DIRECTIONS ON GAME BOARD: (two players) Roll die and move that number of places on board. If you land on a number card, multiply the number on the card by the number on the die. If correct, stay there. If incorrect, go back to where you were. Remember that an ace is equal to one. When you land on a face card, take another turn. The first player to reach the *Card Whiz* space is the winner.

ADDITIONAL ACTIVITIES: This game can be used for addition and subtraction facts as well as for identifying the numbers before or after.

CHECKMATE

SKILL: Multiplication—Facts, *0–9* tables

PURPOSE: To be able to recall the products of the multiplication tables for *0–9.*

Note: The *product* is the answer in multiplication.

MATERIALS: Poster board (18″ × 18″) or checkerboard, checker pieces.

CONSTRUCTION OF GAME BOARD: Draw a checkerboard on poster board or use one you have. In each space write a number *0* to *9* in random order. On each checker also write a number *0* to *9.*

DIRECTIONS ON GAME BOARD: Play checkers the usual way, but before you move to another space or jump a player, you must multiply the number on the board by the number on the checker.

ADDITIONAL ACTIVITIES: Instead of multiplying, have the learner add or subtract the number on the checker with the number on the board.

Use buttons if checker pieces are not available.

Use other commercial board games and substitute the commercial cards for ones you make to reinforce a specific skill.

NUMBER BOARD

SKILL: Multiplication—Facts, *5* table

PURPOSE: To be able to recall the products of the multiplication table for *5.*

Note: The *product* is the answer in multiplication.

MATERIALS: Poster board (12″ × 18″ and 9″ × 12″).

CONSTRUCTION OF GAME BOARD: Make a large outline of the number *5* on the poster board. Divide it into sections to form a game course. Mark *Start* and *Finish* on the course.

From the other sheet of poster board, make multiplication fact cards to correspond to the number. For example, the game cards for this game should be for the *5* table in multiplication.

Provide a die and markers.

DIRECTIONS ON GAME BOARD: (two players) Put markers on *Start.* In turn, draw a card and give answer. If correct, roll die and move that number of places on board. If answer is incorrect, do not move. The first player to reach *Finish* is the winner.

ADDITIONAL ACTIVITIES: Similar game courses can be made for any number *1* to *9* to provide drill in that particular table.

MOUSE ON THE RUN

SKILL: Money—Word Problems—Addition and Subtraction

PURPOSE: The learner will be able to solve word problems with amounts of money.

MATERIALS: Poster board (24″ × 36″), magazine pictures, index cards (3″ × 5″), string-tie envelope.

CONSTRUCTION OF GAME BOARD: On the outer edge of the poster board, draw or paste magazine pictures that, when drawn or arranged, tell a story. Connect the pictures with arrows to form a game course and include a beginning and end on the course.

On the cards, write money word problems that pertain to the pictures and tell a story about the pictures. Number each card.

Sample money problems for cards include:

- Mouse left the house to go on a vacation and took $125.00.
- Mouse stopped at the cheese store to buy some cheese for $3.95 a pound and bought two pounds. How much money did Mouse spend and how much money is left?
- While driving along, Mouse took some pictures of the sights. Mouse bought film that cost $1.98. How much money is left?
- Mouse needed gas and filled the tank for $10.23. How much money is now left?
- Mouse finally arrived at the Hotel and stayed two nights. Each night cost $23.00. After paying for the room, how much vacation money is left?
- The next day Mouse went for a helicopter and canoe ride. The helicopter ride was $8.50 and the canoe ride was $4.75. What is the total price of the two rides? How much money is left?
- The last day of the vacation was spent relaxing on the beach. Mouse spent $2.19 for suntan oil. How much money does Mouse take home?

To make the game board self-checking, the amount of money left at the end of the journey can be provided on an answer key for the learner to compare.

Store cards and answer key in a string-tie envelope attached to the back of the game board.

DIRECTIONS ON GAME BOARD: (one player) Put marker on *Start* and take the first card. Follow all directions on the card and move the marker on the game board as each problem is solved. Do your work on paper.

ADDITIONAL ACTIVITIES: Themes for other story boards include:

Shopping at the Mall
Grocery Store Spree
Amusement Park Adventure
A Trip to the Historical City
Feature Attraction
Sport Spectacular

SHOPPING SPREE

SKILL: Money—Dollars and Cents

PURPOSE: To be able to read amounts of money to $5.00.

MATERIALS: Poster board (18″ × 24″), supermarket advertisements, paper clip, paper brad.

CONSTRUCTION OF GAME BOARD: On the poster board make a game course in the shape of the letter *S.* Divide the course into sections and in most sections cut and paste a picture of a different food item. (Supermarket advertisements are good sources for pictures.) Also include a price for each item written in dollars and cents. (Examples: $1.10, $ .79, $ .55)

On designated sections of the game course write reward statements. (Examples: Go ahead 2 spaces. Take another turn.) Call these sections *Coupons.* At the beginning of the course write *Enter* and at the end *Check Out.*

Make a paper-clip spinner on the game board by inserting a paper brad through a paper clip and affixing it to a corner of the poster board.

Write the directions on the game board.

DIRECTIONS ON GAME BOARD: (two players) Put markers on *Enter.* In turn, spin spinner, move that number of places on the board, and read the price of the item. Follow directions for coupon box when you land there. The first player to reach *Check Out* is the winner.

ADDITIONAL ACTIVITIES: To increase difficulty, the learner can subtract from $5.00 the amount for each item landed on and indicate the change.

A variation of this game is to have each player keep a running tally of the amounts for each item landed upon. The winner is the player who spends the most money.

TIME MARCHES ON

SKILL: Telling Time—Hour, Half-Hour

PURPOSE: Given a specific time, the learner will be able to set a clock to the hour or half-hour.

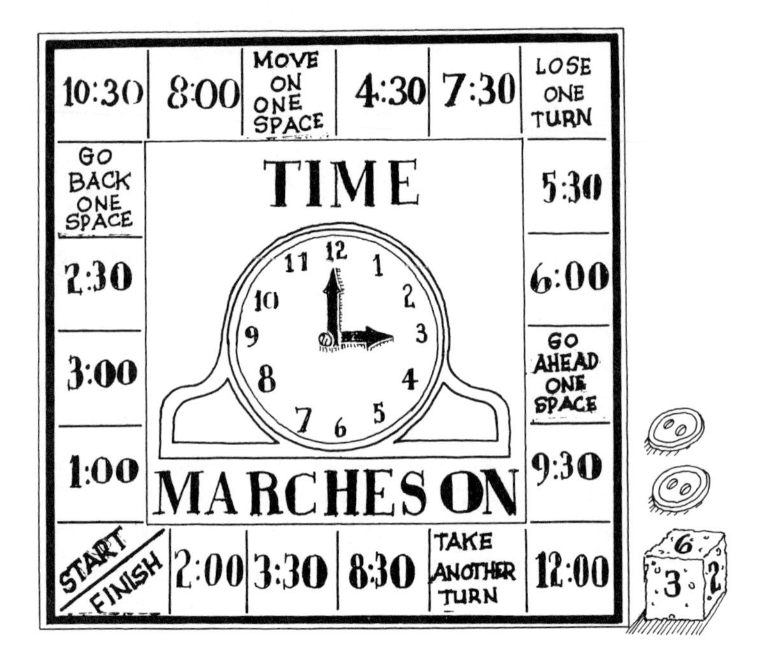

MATERIALS: Poster board (24″ × 24″ and 9″ × 12″), paper brad.

CONSTRUCTION OF GAME BOARD: Make a clock face in the center of the poster board. Attach hands with a paper brad.

Section off a game course around the outside edge of the game board. In various sections write clock times. (Examples: 8:00, 12:00, 2:30, and so on.) Include a space on the course for *Start* and *Finish.*

In designated sections on the course write reward or penalty moves. (Examples: Go back one space. Take another turn.)

Provide a die and markers for the game.

DIRECTIONS ON GAME BOARD: (two players) In turn, roll die and move that number of places on the board. Set the clock in the center of the board for the time on the space or follow the directions on the space. If correct, stay there. If incorrect, go back to where you were. The first player to reach *Finish* is the winner.

ADDITIONAL ACTIVITIES: Construct a clock using a paper plate to use for further drill.

A similar game course can be designed for quarter-hour and five-minute interval times.

DRAG RACE

SKILL: Measurement—Inch, Half-Inch

PURPOSE: The learner will be able to measure to the nearest inch or half-inch.

MATERIALS: Poster board (24″ × 36″), index card (3″ × 5″), paper clip, paper brad.

CONSTRUCTION OF GAME BOARD: Draw three or four evenly spaced vertical lines on the poster board and use these as the game courses. Leave a one-inch margin on each end and mark one end *Start* and the other end *Finish.* Divide and mark each game course into half-inch segments from start to finish.

Make a paper-clip spinner by cutting an index card into a 3″-square. Insert a paper brad through a paper clip and attach it to the center of the card. Divide the card into six to eight sections and in each section write such measurement lengths as 1½″, 3½″, 2½″, 5″, 4″, 1″.

Unique markers for the game can be toy cars. Each player will need a ruler.

DIRECTIONS ON GAME BOARD: (two to four players) Choose a game course. Place markers on *Start.* In turn, spin spinner and measure that distance with a ruler. Place markers there. The first player to reach *Finish* is the winner.

ADDITIONAL ACTIVITIES: Design a similar game using quarter-inch or eighth-inch line segments on the course.

Divide the courses into centimeters and have the learner measure to the nearer centimeter.

CALENDAR WALK

SKILL: Reading a Calendar

PURPOSE: The learner will be able to use the calendar to locate various days of the week and month.

MATERIALS: Poster board (24″ × 36″ and 12″ × 18″), calendar.

CONSTRUCTION OF GAME BOARD: Paste one or more calendar months on poster board. These will be used for the game course. On designated spaces write statements that instruct players to move to certain locations on the months.

Sample moves include:

Move to the third Sunday of the month.
Move to the second Tuesday.
Go to the 18th of the month.
Go to the 24th of the month.

On the other spaces, write the word *Card.* Use the smaller sheet of poster board to make a set of cards. On each card write a statement instructing players to move to a certain location on the board.

Decorate the game board with seasonal pictures.

DIRECTIONS ON GAME BOARD: (two to four players) In turn, roll die, move that number of places on game board, and follow directions on that space. If you land on a *Card* space, take a card and follow the directions on it. The first player to reach the last day of the last calendar month on the game board is the winner.

ADDITIONAL ACTIVITIES: The cards can be extended to include facts pertaining to months, weeks, and days. (Examples: How many days are in one week?; How many weeks are in one year?; What holiday in November makes you think of the Pilgrims?)

AWAY WE GO

SKILL: Multipurpose

PURPOSE: By playing the game, the learner will be able to reinforce a particular skill depending upon need.

MATERIALS: Poster board (24″ × 36″ and 12″ × 18″), paper clip, paper brad.

CONSTRUCTION OF GAME BOARD: Draw the back of an old-fashioned car with a large tire covering the trunk on the poster board. Make a spiral game course in the tire. Mark *Start* and *Finish* on the course. On several spaces mark reward and penalty moves.

Sample moves include:

Pass a slow car. (Move ahead two spaces.)
Got a flat tire. (Lose one turn.)
Missed the turn. (Go back two spaces.)

Affix a paper-clip spinner to the game board by inserting a paper brad through a paper clip and attaching it to a 3″ × 3″ corner of the game board.

Include markers and cards for the specific skill to be reinforced.

DIRECTIONS ON GAME BOARD: (two players) Place markers on *Start* and put cards face down. In turn, draw a card, give answer, spin, and move that number of places on spinner if answer is correct. If answer is incorrect, player does not move. Also, follow all directions on the course. The first player to reach *Finish* is the winner.

ADDITIONAL ACTIVITIES: The game is multipurpose, therefore it can be used for a variety of skills such as recognizing common road signs and symbols and learning safety rules.

ON A SAFARI

SKILL: Multipurpose

PURPOSE: By playing the game, the learner will be able to reinforce a particular skill depending upon need.

MATERIALS: Poster board (24″ × 36″ and 9″ × 12″), wild animal pictures, animal stickers, paper clip, paper brad.

CONSTRUCTION OF GAME BOARD: Cut and paste wild animal pictures onto the large poster board. (Nature magazines contain pictures that are good to use.) Use animal stickers to form the game course. Around designated stickers write reward or penalty moves.

Sample moves include:

Spot a lion. (Jump ahead three spaces.)
Dropped your map. (Go back to start for a new one.)
Got stuck in quicksand. (Lose one turn.)
Stopped to eat a banana. (Lose one turn.)

In the upper right-hand corner draw a 3″ × 3″ square and construct a paper-clip spinner by inserting a paper brad through a paper clip and attaching it to the center of the square. Divide into sections and write the numbers *1* to *3* in each section.

Make cards from the small sheet of poster board and write words or examples depending upon the particular skill you are reinforcing.

DIRECTIONS ON GAME BOARD: (two players) Go on a safari by playing this game. Put cards face down. In turn, spin spinner, draw a card, give answer, and move the number of places on spinner if answer is correct. If answer is incorrect, do not move. The first player to reach *Finish* is the winner.

ADDITIONAL ACTIVITIES: Skill cards can be made for reinforcement of classification of animals (mammals, reptiles, amphibians).

Instead of using animal stickers, use cutout safari hats as the game course.

OLYMPIC CHAMP

SKILL: Multipurpose

PURPOSE: By playing the game, the learner will be able to reinforce a particular skill depending upon need.

MATERIALS: Poster board (24″ × 24″ and 12″ × 18″), construction paper, sports pictures, string-tie envelope.

CONSTRUCTION OF GAME BOARD: Make a large *X*, 2½″ wide, going from corner to corner on the poster board. In the center of the *X* glue three cutout medals (gold, silver, bronze). In each corner space write *Start* for individual game courses. Decorate the game board with sports pictures.

Provide cards for the specific skill to be reinforced, markers, and die. Store in a string-tie envelope attached to the back of the game board.

DIRECTIONS ON GAME BOARD: (two or four players) Be a champ and win a gold, silver, or bronze medal. Put markers on individual game courses and cards face down. In turn, draw a card, give answer, roll die, and move that number of places on individual course if answer is correct. If incorrect, do not move. Continue playing until a player reaches the *Gold Medal* and is the Gold Medal Winner. Then the remaining players continue playing until there is a (*Silver Medal*) second place and (*Bronze Medal*) third place winner.

ADDITIONAL ACTIVITIES: Write sports words on cards and have the learner reinforce such skills as syllabication, vowel sounds, or recognizing nouns and verbs.

CAMP-OUT

SKILL: Multipurpose

PURPOSE: By playing the game, the learner will be able to reinforce a particular skill depending upon need.

MATERIALS: Poster board (24″ × 36″ and 12″ × 18″), coding label dots, magazine pictures, paper clip, paper brad.

CONSTRUCTION OF GAME BOARD: Make a game course on the large poster board by using coding label dots or making your own from construction paper. Around the game course draw pictures or use magazine pictures of camping experiences. (Examples: tent, sports activities, flag raising, canoe race.) On designated dots write reward, penalty, and location moves.

Sample moves include:

Started camp fire. (Move ahead one space.)
Burned a marshmallow. (Go back one space.)
Got bit by mosquitoes. (Go back to tent for repellent.)
Fell in lake. (Lose one turn to dry off.)

Attach a paper-clip spinner to the game board and include cards for the specific skill to be reinforced.

DIRECTIONS ON GAME BOARD: (two to four players) Put cards face down. In turn, spin spinner, draw card, give answer, and move that number of places on board if answer is correct. If answer is incorrect, do not move. The first player to reach *Finish* is the winner.

ADDITIONAL ACTIVITIES: Make true-and-false cards for such skills as safety and good health habits.

Use cutout paper stones or leaves as a game course instead of coding label dots.

MANIPULATIVE DEVICES THAT MATTER

BUTTERFLY MATCH

SKILL: Color—Recognition

PURPOSE: The learner will be able to match colors to the color word.

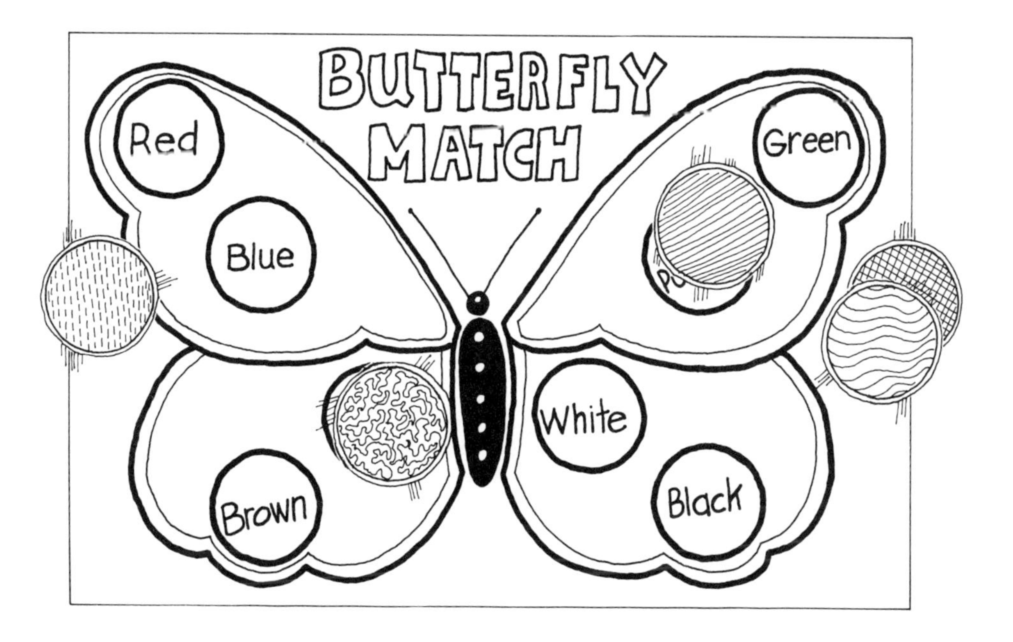

MATERIALS: Poster board (24″ × 36″), construction paper, string-tie envelope.

CONSTRUCTION OF MANIPULATIVE DEVICE: Draw a butterfly on the poster board. On the butterfly wings outline eight circles, 4″ in diameter, and in each circle write a color word.

Cut other circles from construction paper the same size as those on the board. Use colors named in the circles on the butterfly. Store the circles in a string-tie envelope attached to the back of the manipulative device.

Directions on Manipulative Device: Help make the butterfly beautiful. Take the colored circles out of the envelope and match them to the color words on the board.

Additional Activities: Match the colored circles with objects in the classroom or home.

Place small objects on the color words on the butterfly.

Cut pictures from magazines that are a specific color and paste on paper to form a color collage.

SPOT A CLOWN

Skill: Capital and Lowercase Letters

Purpose: The learner will be able to match capital letters to the corresponding lowercase letter.

Materials: Poster board (12″ × 18″), construction paper, string-tie envelope.

Construction of Manipulative Device: On poster board, draw and cut out a clown face with a large pointed hat. On the hat draw circles and in each write a lowercase letter.

Cut out other circles the same size as those on the clown and on each write a capital letter for those on the hat.

Store the circles in a string-tie envelope attached to the back of the clown. Write the directions on the envelope.

Directions on Manipulative Device: Decorate the clown's hat by matching the capital letters to the lowercase letters.

Additional Activities: Toss a small rubber eraser on the clown's hat and identify the letter.

Toss a small rubber eraser on the clown's hat and identify the letter that comes before and after.

Practice writing the lowercase and capital letters on paper, chalkboard, or sand table.

In place of the circles with letters, make other circles that have a picture or word that begins with a letter on the clown. Have the learner match these.

APPLE PICKING TIME

SKILL: Alphabetical Order

PURPOSE: To be able to recognize the order of the letters of the alphabet.

MATERIALS: Poster board (24″ × 36″), construction paper.

CONSTRUCTION OF MANIPULATIVE DEVICE: Paste a tree, cut from construction paper, onto the poster board. Paste eight to ten construction-paper apples on the tree. On each apple write a letter of the alphabet.

Cut several more apples the same size as those on the tree. On these, write a letter of the alphabet that comes before each letter on the tree. Store the apples in a basket-shaped pocket affixed near the tree and write the directions on the basket.

DIRECTIONS ON MANIPULATIVE DEVICE: Look at the apples on the tree. Place the apples in the basket on top of the apples on the tree if the letter on the apple comes before those on the tree.

ADDITIONAL ACTIVITIES: Vary the directions by making other apples with letters that come after those on the tree or make apples that have a picture of a word that begins with a letter on the tree.

FLYING HIGH

SKILL: Alphabetizing

PURPOSE: Given a selected group of words, the learner will be able to write them in alphabetical order according to their first and second letters.

Note: When putting words in alphabetical order, look at the first letter of each word and arrange them according to the sequence of the alphabet. If words have the same first letter, look at the second letter and place them alphabetically according to the second letter.

MATERIALS: Poster board (12″ × 18″), yarn, construction paper, string-tie envelope.

CONSTRUCTION OF MANIPULATIVE DEVICE: Cut a kite from the poster board and attach a piece of yarn for the tail. Make bows from the poster board and write a word on each.

Sample words include:

blow	colorful	high	sky
breeze	fly	mild	tree
clouds	glide	pole	wind

Make several small kites from construction paper.

Store bows and paper kites in a string-tie envelope attached to the back of the kite. Write the directions on the envelope.

DIRECTIONS ON MANIPULATIVE DEVICE: Take the bows out of the envelope and place them on the yarn in alphabetical order. Take a paper kite and write the words in alphabetical order. Decorate the other side of the kite and attach a tail.

ADDITIONAL ACTIVITIES: Write a story about a kite. Title it *Flying High,* and use the words on the bows in the story.

SPOT A LADYBUG

SKILL: Vowel Sounds—Long and Short

PURPOSE: Given a selected word, the learner will be able to identify the vowel sound as long or short.

Note: A vowel is usually short if a word or syllable has one vowel at the beginning or between two consonants. If a word has two vowels, the first vowel is usually long and the second one is silent.

MATERIALS: Poster board (18″ × 24″), black construction paper, string-tie envelope.

CONSTRUCTION OF MANIPULATIVE DEVICE: Cut two large ladybugs from the poster board. Make several black cutout circles and with white crayon write a word containing a long or short vowel sound on each.

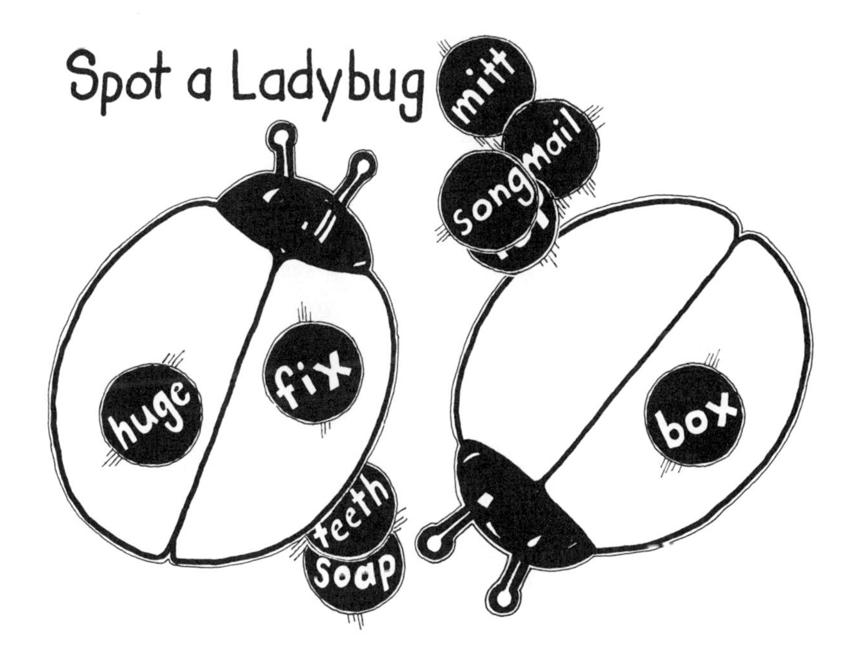

Sample words include:

Short Vowel Sounds		
trap	grab	bug
chick	then	rust
mitt	fix	box

Long Vowel Sounds		
mail	wave	teeth
huge	heat	slide
price	stone	soap

Store circles in a string-tie envelope attached to the back of one of the ladybugs. Write the directions on the envelope. For storage, clip the ladybugs together with a clothespin.

DIRECTIONS ON MANIPULATIVE DEVICE: (two players) Each player chooses a ladybug. Put the circles face down. In turn, a player takes a circle, reads the word, and tells if the vowel sound is long or short. If correct, the circle is put on the player's ladybug. After all the circle cards are used, the winner is the player with the most circles on the ladybug.

ADDITIONAL ACTIVITIES: Choose ten words written on the circles and write a sentence for each.

Think of and list five words with a long vowel sound and five words with a short vowel sound.

BUZZING AROUND

SKILL: Vowel Sounds—Long and Short—*u*

PURPOSE: Given a selected word with the vowel *u* in it, the learner will be able to identify it as long or short.

Note: A vowel is usually short if a word or syllable has one vowel at the beginning or between two consonants. If a word has two vowels, the first vowel is usually long and the second one is silent.

MATERIALS: Poster board (24″ × 36″), construction paper, one index card (3″ × 5″), string-tie envelope.

CONSTRUCTION OF MANIPULATIVE DEVICE: Cut two large flowers from different colors of construction paper. In the center of one write *short* and in the other write *long*. On the poster board draw stems (one short and one long) and leaves for the flowers. Glue the flower that says *short* on the short stem and the flower that says *long* on the long stem.

Make several cutout bees and on each write a word that is long or short.

Sample words include:

Short Vowel Sounds		*Long Vowel Sounds*	
buzz	jug	huge	rule
pump	mud	cube	flute
rust	cub	cute	mule

Draw and cut out a hive from the index card. Use this as an answer key and title it *Bee Keeper.* Store bees and answer key in a string-tie envelope attached to the back of the poster board.

DIRECTIONS ON MANIPULATIVE DEVICE: Look at the words on the bees. If the word has a short vowel sound, put it near the flower with the short stem. If the word has a long vowel sound, put it near the flower with the long stem. Check your work with the *Bee Keeper* card when you have finished.

ADDITIONAL ACTIVITIES: Make additional cutout bee cards for other vowel sounds.

PERKY PEACOCK

SKILL: Regular Double Vowel—*ea*

PURPOSE: The learner will be able to identify the *ea* sound in a word.

Note: A regular double vowel occurs when two vowels come together in a word and the first is usually long and the second is silent. (Example: bead) A vowel digraph or irregular double vowel occurs when two vowels come together in a word and the first is short and the second is silent. (Example: spread)

MATERIALS: Poster board (24″ × 36″), construction paper, string-tie envelope.

CONSTRUCTION OF MANIPULATIVE DEVICE: On the poster board draw and color a peacock.

Cut out several oval-shaped spots from construction paper and on each write a word containing *ea.*

Sample words include:

Regular Double Vowels			*Irregular Double Vowels*		
eagle	cream	creak	health	feather	treasure
peak	leaves	seal	thread	sweater	spread

Write answers (regular double vowel words) on a large oval-shaped paper and store spots and answer key in a string-tie envelope attached to the back of the manipulative device.

DIRECTIONS ON MANIPULATIVE DEVICE: Help perk up Perky Peacock's tail by putting the spots, which have the *ea* sound as in peacock, on the tail. Check your answers when you have finished.

ADDITIONAL ACTIVITIES: Make additional spots for other regular double vowels such as *ei* and *ie.*

VOWEL OWL

SKILL: Diphthongs—*ow*

PURPOSE: The learner will be able to identify the *ow* sound in a word.

Note: A *diphthong* occurs when two vowels blend together so that they both are heard as one sound. (Example: *owl*) Sometimes *ow* is a regular double vowel and can have a long vowel sound. (Example: *slow*)

MATERIALS: Poster board (24″ × 36″), construction paper, one index card (3″ × 5″), string-tie envelope.

CONSTRUCTION OF MANIPULATIVE DEVICE: Draw an owl on the poster board.

From construction paper make and cut out several feathers. On each feather write a word with the *ow* sound.

Sample words include:

Diphthongs		*Regular Double Vowels*	
owl	power	low	show
cow	shower	blow	growth
towel	flower	elbow	snow

Write the answers (diphthongs) on the index card and store answer card and feathers in a string-tie envelope attached to the back of the poster board.

DIRECTIONS ON MANIPULATIVE DEVICE: Take the feathers out of the envelope and read each word. If the word has an *ow* sound as in *owl,* put the feather on the owl's body. Check your answers when you have finished.

ADDITIONAL ACTIVITIES: Record the words on a tape recorder and listen to the *ow* sound when it is played back.

Make additional feathers for the diphthongs *ou, oi, oy,* and *ew.*

SHIP AHOY!

SKILL: Rhyming Words

PURPOSE: The learner will be able to match beginning consonants to the ending of a word and form new words that rhyme.

Note: Words that rhyme sound the same in their ending sounds.

MATERIALS: Poster board (24″ × 36″ and 9″ × 12″), string tie envelope.

CONSTRUCTION OF MANIPULATIVE DEVICE: On the poster board draw a ship with poles for sails, but do not draw the sails. At the top of each pole draw a flag. Label them *ill, ack, ook,* respectively.

Use the small piece of poster board to make the sails (2″ × 3″). On each sail write a beginning consonant(s).

Sample beginning consonants and ending sounds include:

ill	*ack*	*ook*
fill	sack	book
hill	tack	look
mill	back	took
pill	pack	hook
drill	track	brook
spill	crack	shook

Make an answer key on a cutout anchor. Put the sails and answer key in a string-tie envelope attached to the back of the manipulative device. Write the directions on the envelope.

DIRECTIONS ON MANIPULATIVE DEVICE: Make rhyming words by putting the sails on either the *ill, ack,* or *ook* pole. Check your answers by looking on the anchor when finished.

ADDITIONAL ACTIVITIES: For additional use of the manipulative device, laminate or cover it with clear self-adhesive paper and write the word endings with a grease pencil.

Make additional sails for other rhyming words.

Make "rhyming mobiles" using cutout hooks and fish. Write the word ending on the hook and have the learner write words that rhyme on fish. The learner can then match and affix the fish to the hooks.

MAKE A WISH

SKILL: Initial and Final Consonant Blends—*st*
PURPOSE: The learner will be able to make words containing the initial and final consonant blend *st*.

Note: A *consonant blend* is formed when two or more consonants are together and each sound is heard.

MATERIALS: Poster board (12″ × 18″ and 9″ × 12″), yarn.

CONSTRUCTION OF MANIPULATIVE DEVICE: Draw a wishing well on the large sheet of poster board. Make a ½″-slit at the top center of the well base and at the top of the well.

Make a yarn pully with a pail attached. This is done by affixing a cutout pail to a piece of yarn. Then put it through the slits and tie it in the back.

On the pail write the blend *st.* Along the right side of the poster board, where the pail is pulled up, write the endings of words that begin with *st* and on the left side write beginnings of words that end in *st.*

Sample endings and beginnings of words include:

Endings of Words		*Beginnings of Words*	
store	stage	toast	vest
star	state	mast	coast
steep	stand	cast	west

DIRECTIONS ON MANIPULATIVE DEVICE: Make a wish by pulling up the pail and saying each new word you make.

ADDITIONAL ACTIVITIES: Use each word in a sentence.

Think of other words with the *st* blend.

Make a wish and write a paragraph telling about your wish and why you want it. Use five of the words around the wishing well in the paragraph.

UNDER THE BIG TOP

SKILL: Initial Consonant Blends—*tr, fl, sn*

PURPOSE: To be able to make new words by matching a consonant blend to an incomplete word.

Note: A *consonant blend* is formed when two or more consonants are together and each sound is heard.

MATERIALS: Poster board (24″ × 36″), three small cardboard discs, 9″ in diameter (pizza discs are good to use), circus pictures or stickers.

CONSTRUCTION OF MANIPULATIVE DEVICE: On the poster board, draw an outline of a circus tent. Attach two or three small discs with paper brads to serve as the circus rings. To the left of each disc write a consonant blend and on each disc write incomplete words that when added to the blend will form words.

Sample blends and words include:

tr	*fl*	*sn*
__ip	__oor	__ore
__ay	__ag	__eeze
__ain	__ood	__ow
__uck	__y	__eak
__ap	__at	__ail
__ail	__ip	__ake

Decorate the manipulative device with circus pictures or stickers.

DIRECTIONS ON MANIPULATIVE DEVICE: Turn each circus ring to form new words. Say each word and write it on paper.

ADDITIONAL ACTIVITIES: Do some creative writing. Write a story about the circus. Title it *Under the Big Top.* Include at least one word from each disc in your story.

Make additional discs with other incomplete words to affix to the board.

IT'S THE JUGGLING JUGGLER

SKILL: Contractions

PURPOSE: Given a selected contraction, the learner will be able to identify the two words it stands for.

Note: A *contraction* is a short way of writing two words. One or more letters are left out and an apostrophe is put in its place.

MATERIALS: Poster board (24″ × 36″ and 12″ × 18″), construction paper, string-tie envelope.

CONSTRUCTION OF MANIPULATIVE DEVICE: On poster board draw and color a juggler with a juggling pin on top of the head. Put the hands of the juggler in the air. Make a stripe about 1½″-wide on the pin.

From poster board make cards the width and length of the stripe on the pin and write a contraction on each.

Sample contractions for the cards include:

didn't	I'd	we're
wouldn't	I'm	they're
isn't	let's	it's

Make 4″ × 4″ squares and put one word from a contraction on each.
Sample words for squares, from which contractions are formed, include:

did not	I would, I had	we are
would not	I am	they are
is not	let us	it is

Cut 4″ × 4″ squares from construction paper to use as the learner's work papers.

Store the pieces of the activity in a string-tie envelope attached to the back of the manipulative device.

DIRECTIONS ON MANIPULATIVE DEVICE: Help the juggler juggle the squares. Put a contraction card on the stripe on the pin. In the hands put squares that mean the same as the card. Each time you do this, write your answers on the work paper.

ADDITIONAL ACTIVITIES: Instead of using this activity for contractions, make cards and squares for addition, subtraction, multiplication, or division facts and answers. In the pin place the answer and in the hands the two numbers that equal it.

SPOT THE TURTLE

SKILL: Homonyms

PURPOSE: Given selected words, the learner will be able to match each word to its corresponding homonym.

Note: A *homonym* is a word that sounds the same, but is spelled differently and has a different meaning.

MATERIALS: Poster board (12″ × 18″ and 9″ × 12″), string-tie envelope.

CONSTRUCTION OF MANIPULATIVE DEVICE: Draw and cut out a turtle from the poster board. On the shell of the turtle draw circles (spots) and in each circle write a homonym.

From a different color of poster board, cut out several circles to match the spots on the turtle. On each of these circles write a homonym to match the ones on the turtle.

Sample homonyms for turtle and cutout spots include:

for—four
bluc—blew
road—rode
pear—pare

piece—peace
hour—our
sent—cent
to—two

sea—see
dear—deer
knew—new
hair—hare

Write answers on a large circle and store spots and answer key in a string-tie envelope attached to the back of the turtle.

DIRECTIONS ON MANIPULATIVE DEVICE: Each circle in the envelope contains a homonym. Match the circle to the correct homonym on the turtle. Check your answers with the answer key.

ADDITIONAL ACTIVITIES: Draw a picture to represent the meaning of each homonym. (Examples: "mailing a letter" for *sent;* "some coins" for *cent.*) Write a sentence under each picture using the homonym.

COMPOUND CONFUSION

SKILL: Compound Words

PURPOSE: To be able to match two words together to form a compound word.

Note: A *compound word* is made up of two words put together to make one.

MATERIALS: Poster board (12″ × 18″), string-tie envelope.

CONSTRUCTION OF MANIPULATIVE DEVICE: Cut the poster board into 3″ × 5″ strips. In a zig-zag fashion, cut each strip in half. On one half, write one word from a compound word and on the other half write the other. Store pieces in a string-tie envelope.

DIRECTIONS ON MANIPULATIVE DEVICE: Take the pieces out of the envelope and match the halves to form compound words.

ADDITIONAL ACTIVITIES: Instead of cutting the poster board in a zig-zag fashion, paste a small picture on the back of each card and then cut the picture along with the card in half. The learner can self-check by seeing if the pictures are put together correctly.

UNDERWATER DIVE

SKILL: Syllabication—1, 2, 3 Syllable Words

PURPOSE: Given a selected word, the learner will be able to tell how many syllables are in the word.

Note: A *syllable* is a word or part of a word that contains a vowel sound.

MATERIALS: Poster board (18″ × 24″), construction paper, string-tie envelope.

CONSTRUCTION OF MANIPULATIVE DEVICE: Draw an underwater diver on the poster board.

Make and cut out several fish from various colors of construction paper. On each fish write a word.

Sample words include:

One-Syllable Words	*Two-Syllable Words*	*Three-Syllable Words*
fish	diver	submarine
snail	goggles	hurricane
surf	treasure	octopus
moss	ocean	jellyfish
shell	bubbles	tentacle

On cutout goggles, write answers and store fish and goggle answer key in a string-tie envelope attached to the back of the manipulative device.

DIRECTIONS ON MANIPULATIVE DEVICE: (two players) Put the fish all around the diver. One player plays while the other checks the answers. Later the players switch positions. The player draws a fish (one at a time), says the word on the fish and the number of syllables in the word until a mistake is made or the player answers all the fish cards correctly. When finished, the player counts the number of fish in hand. The fish are then replaced around the diver for the other player. When both players have had their turn, the winner of the game is the one who has had the most fish.

ADDITIONAL ACTIVITIES: Color code the fish so that different fish can be used for different skills. (Examples: red fish for syllabication, blue fish for compound words, yellow fish for multiplication facts, and so on.) Then, this same activity can be used for a variety of skill areas.

WORD SORT

SKILL: Prefixes—*re, de, un*

PURPOSE: To be able to make new words by adding the prefix *re, de,* or *un* to a root word.

Note: A *prefix* is a syllable added to the beginning of a root word forming a new word. The prefix changes the meaning of the word. A *root word* is the word to which the prefix is added.

MATERIALS: Three frozen juice cans, wooden craft sticks, construction paper, index card (3″ × 5″).

CONSTRUCTION OF MANIPULATIVE DEVICE: Obtain frozen juice cans and fifteen to twenty wooden craft sticks. Cover the cans with colored paper and on each write a prefix. On each stick write a root word.

Sample prefixes and root words include:

re	*de*	*un*
__open	__frost	__cover
__copy	__rail	__load
__tell	__part	__safe
__fill	__press	__fair
__bound	__light	__hurt

Write the directions on one of the cans. Use the card as an answer key and store it inside the can with the directions.

DIRECTIONS ON MANIPULATIVE DEVICE: Make a new word by putting the sticks in the right can. Check your work with the answer key when you have finished.

ADDITIONAL ACTIVITIES: Compare the meaning of the words for one of the prefixes. Fold a piece of paper in half. On the left, write the root word and its meaning and on the right the new word along with its meaning. Compare the differences.

THE LONG AND SHORT OF IT

SKILL: Abbreviations

PURPOSE: To be able to match the abbreviations of a word to the word it represents.

Note: An *abbreviation* is a shortened form of a word.

MATERIALS: Poster board (9″ × 12″), yarn.

CONSTRUCTION OF MANIPULATIVE DEVICE: On the poster board draw six or more evenly spaced horizontal lines. Divide these in half vertically. In the left column, write the abbreviations for selected words. In the right column, in random order, write the words for the abbreviations.

Sample words and abbreviations include:

Mister—Mr.	Doctor—Dr.	Avenue—Ave.
Street—St.	Road—Rd.	Pound—lb.
Building—bldg.	Monday—Mon.	January—Jan.

Attach yarn next to each abbreviation by making a small hole and tying it in the back with a knot. Cut a ½″-slit in the middle of each box on the right edge of the poster board. On the back of the card, next to each slit, write the abbreviations for self-checking.

DIRECTIONS ON MANIPULATIVE DEVICE: Match the abbreviation and the word it represents by putting the yarn in the correct slit. Check your answers by looking on the back of the card.

ADDITIONAL ACTIVITIES: Other cards with this slit technique can be made for homonyms, synonyms, antonyms, states and capital cities, and math facts.

PUZZLE MATCH-UP

SKILL: Nouns and Verbs

PURPOSE: Given selected words, the learner will be able to recognize the difference between words that are nouns and words that are verbs.

Note: A *noun* is a word that names a person, place, or thing. A *verb* is a word that shows action or is a word of being.

MATERIALS: Two plastic lids (coffee can lids are good to use), construction paper, string-tie envelope.

CONSTRUCTION OF MANIPULATIVE DEVICE: Obtain two plastic lids from empty coffee cans. Label one lid *nouns* and the other *verbs.*

Puzzle Match-Up

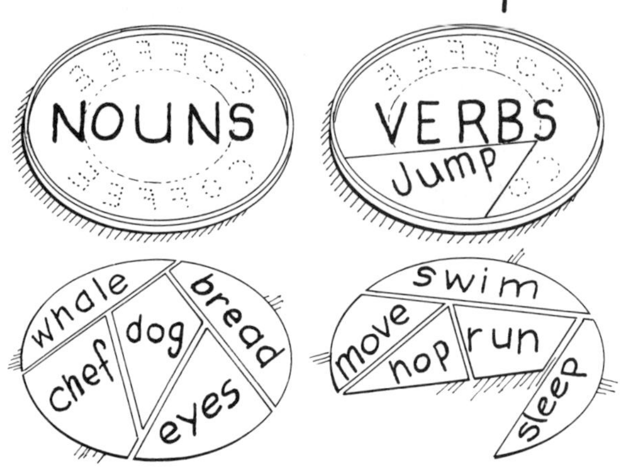

Cut out two circles from construction paper the same size as the lids. Divide and cut each into six to eight sections. On the sections of one circle write words that are nouns and on the sections of the other, write words that are verbs.

Sample nouns and verbs include:

Nouns		*Verbs*	
chef	dog	walk	jump
whale	children	run	talk
bread	subway	hop	move
hobby	eyes	drive	sleep

Store lids and pieces in a string-tie envelope.

DIRECTIONS ON MANIPULATIVE DEVICE: Form puzzles by putting words that are nouns in the *Noun* lid and those that are verbs in the *Verb* lid.

ADDITIONAL ACTIVITIES: To vary the idea, use the plastic coffee scoops found in coffee cans. Write words that are nouns or verbs on the scoops. Label two coffee cans *Nouns* and *Verbs,* respectively. Have the learner sort the scoops into the proper cans.

Paper cutout scoops can be made if plastic scoops are unavailable.

CAPITAL ROLL CALL

SKILL: Map Reading—Capital Cities

PURPOSE: To be able to identify and locate the capital cities of the fifty states.

MATERIALS: Poster board (18″ × 24″), construction paper, string-tie envelope.

CONSTRUCTION OF MANIPULATIVE DEVICE: Outline a map of the United States on the poster board. Write the names of the states on the map.

Make fifty small flags and on each flag write the capital city for each state.

Provide an answer key and store flags and answer key in a string-tie envelope attached to the back of the manipulative device.

DIRECTIONS ON MANIPULATIVE DEVICE: Match the flags with the capital cities on them to the states on the map. Check the answers with the answer key.

SPELLING INSPECTORS

SKILL: Spelling—Identifying Correct and Incorrect

PURPOSE: The learner will be able to differentiate between correct and incorrect spellings of selected words.

MATERIALS: Poster board (12″ × 18″ and 9″ × 12″), paper clip, paper brad, string-tie envelope.

CONSTRUCTION OF MANIPULATIVE DEVICE: Make a paper-clip spinner in the shape of a magnifying lens and place it in the center of the large piece of poster board. To make the spinner, insert a paper brad through a paper clip and attach it to the center of the lens. Divide it into sections and in each section write a number *1* to *5* in random order.

On one side of the poster board, write the word *Correct* and on the other side, write the word *Incorrect.* Rule off a 3″ × 4″ section on the bottom and write the word *Cards* in this box.

Make several cards and on each write a word that is spelled correctly or incorrectly. Store in a string-tie envelope attached to the back.

DIRECTIONS ON MANIPULATIVE DEVICE: (two players) Be a "spelling inspector" by playing this game. Put the cards face down. In turn, draw a card. If you think the word is spelled correctly, put it under the word *Correct.* If you think it is incorrect, put it under the word *Incorrect.* The opponent looks the word up in the dictionary to see if it is under the correct section. If it is correct the player spins the spinner and that number is the score for this turn. Play continues this way until each player has had five turns. The winner is the player with the highest score.

ADDITIONAL ACTIVITIES: Other cards can be made for such skills as syllabication, antonyms, synonyms, or homonyms.

ON TARGET

SKILL: Dictionary Usage

PURPOSE: The learner will be able to locate words in a dictionary.

MATERIALS: Two cardboard discs, 12″ in diameter (pizza discs are good to use), poster board (12″ × 18″), string-tie envelope.

CONSTRUCTION OF MANIPULATIVE DEVICE: Use the cardboard discs to make targets.

Make a set of cards and on each write a word found in the dictionary.

Sample words include:

target	aim	dart	arrow
excited	weather	bow	action
shoot	center	contest	straight

Draw and cut out two arrows from poster board and color them different colors.

Store the activity in a string-tie envelope. Write the directions on the envelope.

DIRECTIONS ON MANIPULATIVE DEVICE: (two players) Each player will need a target, dictionary, and arrow (marker). Put the cards face down. The first card is turned up and each player looks the word up in the dictionary. The first player to find the word moves the arrow one step closer to the center of the target. Play continues the same way until a player reaches the center of the target—*On Target.*

ADDITIONAL ACTIVITIES: Use the dictionary to look up the words on the cards and find the guide words.

Arrange the words on the cards in alphabetical order.

BIRTHDAY SURPRISE

SKILL: Numeration—Number Recognition

PURPOSE: To be able to match numerals with sets of objects.

MATERIALS: 8″ styrofoam disc, poster board (9″ × 12″), sequins, birthday candles.

CONSTRUCTION OF MANIPULATIVE DEVICE: Glue sequins on the styrofoam disc to make it look like a birthday cake.

Cut out and number a set of 1″ × 3″ cards *1* to *9*. On the back of the cards draw the corresponding number of candles.

Provide birthday candles, enough for the numbers on the cards.

DIRECTIONS ON MANIPULATIVE DEVICE: Put a number card on the cake and then put the correct number of candles on the cake. Turn the card over and check your answers.

ADDITIONAL ACTIVITIES: Select five cards. Draw five cakes. Add candles to the cakes according to the numbers on the cards. Turn the cards over to see if you drew the correct number of candles.

Draw a party picture. In the picture include 1 large cake, 2 party horns, 3 balloons, 4 party hats, 5 cup cakes, 6 children, 7 party cups, 8 chairs, and 9 presents.

SHELL HUNT

SKILL: Addition—Facts to *18*

PURPOSE: The learner will be able to add two single-digit numbers to find the sum.

Note: The *sum* is the answer in addition.

MATERIALS: Sea shells, child's sand pail and shovel, construction paper.

CONSTRUCTION OF MANIPULATIVE DEVICE: Gather about twenty to twenty-five shells and with indelible marker write a single-digit number on each. Store in a child's sand pail.

Make shells from construction paper to use for the learner's work papers.

DIRECTIONS ON MANIPULATIVE DEVICE: Go hunting for shells by scooping up two shells at a time. Add the numbers on the shells and write your fact and answer on the paper shell. Continue until you have fifteen facts.

ADDITIONAL ACTIVITIES: Put the shells in numerical order.

Hide the shells and have two or more learners go on a shell hunt. The learners are to add the numbers on the shells they find and the one with the highest total wins.

Use additional shells and write double-digit numbers for the learner to add or subtract.

NUMBER TOSS

SKILL: Addition

PURPOSE: The learner will be able to add two numbers to find the sum.
Note: The *sum* is the answer in addition.

MATERIALS: Poster board (24″ × 24″), two canning jar rubbers.

CONSTRUCTION OF MANIPULATIVE DEVICE: Evenly divide the poster board into one hundred squares. Write the numbers from 1 to 100 in sequence (left to right) in the boxes.

DIRECTIONS ON MANIPULATIVE DEVICE: Put the activity on the floor or a flat surface. Throw the jar rings onto the activity, one at a time, and then add the two numbers. Write each example on paper. Continue with this until you have twenty examples.

ADDITIONAL ACTIVITIES: Multiply the numbers in the jar rubbers.

Round off each number to the nearest ten.

Tell the place value of each number.

Toss one jar ring on the board and tell what number comes before or after.

Use the activity to count by 2, 3, 5, or 10.

FISHING FOR ANSWERS

SKILL: Subtraction—Facts to *18*

PURPOSE: The learner will be able to subtract two numbers to find the difference.

Note: The *difference* is the answer in subtraction.

MATERIALS: Poster board (24″ × 36″), construction paper, string-tie envelope.

CONSTRUCTION OF MANIPULATIVE DEVICE: On the poster board draw a water scene and include a person fishing in a boat with the line and hook in the water.

Make two sets of different color fish-shaped cards and on each write a subtraction fact. Write the answers for the fish cards on the water.

Store fish cards in a string-tie envelope attached to the back of the manipulative device. Write the directions on the envelope.

DIRECTIONS ON MANIPULATIVE DEVICE: (two players) Each player takes a deck of fish cards. In turn, go fishing for answers by drawing a card from your deck and then placing your fish over the right answer on the water. The winner at the end of the game is the player who has the most fish in the water.

ADDITIONAL ACTIVITIES: Make additional fish-shaped cards and cut each in half. Write a subtraction fact on one half and the answer on the other. Have the learner match the pieces.

SOMETHING TO CROW ABOUT

SKILL: Subtraction—Facts to *18*

PURPOSE: The learner will be able to subtract two numbers to find the difference.

Note: The *difference* is the answer in subtraction.

MATERIALS: Poster board (24″ × 36″), construction paper, index card (3″ × 5″), string-tie envelope.

CONSTRUCTION OF MANIPULATIVE DEVICE: Use indelible markers and construction paper to design a large scarecrow on the poster board.

Also make several crows from construction paper and on each write a subtraction fact.

Write answers on the card and store crows and answer key in a string-tie envelope attached to the back of the manipulative device.

DIRECTIONS ON MANIPULATIVE DEVICE: (two players) Chase all the crows away from the scarecrow by giving the correct answer. Place the crows fact-side down on the scarecrow. One player takes the answer key and checks answers while the other player takes a crow and gives the answer. The player continues picking up crows and giving answers until all the crows have been picked up or a mistake is made. The player, giving answers, then counts the crows in hand and the players switch positions. At the end of the game the player who picked up the most crows is the winner.

ADDITIONAL ACTIVITIES: Use the crow cards as drill cards to practice the subtraction facts.

Make other sets of crows for addition facts or multiplication facts.

SILLY SEAHORSE

SKILL: Subtraction—Facts to *18*

PURPOSE: The learner will be able to subtract two numbers to find the difference.

Note: The *difference* is the answer in subtraction.

MATERIALS: Poster board (24″ × 36″ and 9″ × 12″), construction paper, string-tie envelope.

CONSTRUCTION OF MANIPULATIVE DEVICE: Draw a large seahorse on the poster board. Around the seahorse draw many circles (bubbles). In each circle write a subtraction fact.

Cut two different-colored sets of circles to fit over the circles on the board and on each write the answers for the facts on the board.

Store circles in a string-tie envelope attached to the back of the poster board.

DIRECTIONS ON MANIPULATIVE DEVICE: (two players) Each player chooses a set of colored circles. In turn, choose a circle, find fact on board that equals answer on the circle, and cover it with the circle. When all the circles are covered, the player who has the most circles on the board is the winner.

ADDITIONAL ACTIVITIES: Take a set of circles and on paper write the number that comes before and after the number on the circles.

Choose a set of circles and use the numbers on the circles as the difference for subtraction facts you form.

SPIN-A-FLOWER

SKILL: Multiplication Facts

PURPOSE: The learner will be able to multiply two numbers to find the product.

Note: The *product* is the answer in multiplication.

MATERIALS: Two sheets of poster board (9″ × 12″).

CONSTRUCTION OF MANIPULATIVE DEVICE: Cut a flower with several petals from the poster board. With a paper brad attach the flower to the poster board. Write a number at the edge of each petal and on the poster board opposite the petal write a different number. To decorate, add stem, leaves, and grass to the manipulative device.

DIRECTIONS ON MANIPULATIVE DEVICE: Spin the flower and multiply each number near a petal with the number on the petal. Do this until you have twenty facts on your paper.

Additional Activities: Vary the activity by having the learner add or subtract the numbers.

Two- and three-digit numbers can be used in place of single-digit numbers.

BOTTLE CAP MATH

Skill: Multiplication Facts

Purpose: The learner will be able to multiply two numbers to find the product.

Note: The *product* is the answer in multiplication.

Materials: Milk or soda bottle caps, coffee can, patterned self-adhesive paper, index card (3″ × 5″).

Construction of Manipulative Device: Gather twenty to twenty-five bottle caps. On the top of each write a multiplication fact. Inside the cap write the answer. Store the caps in a coffee can covered with patterned self-adhesive paper.

Write the directions for the activity on the card.

Directions on Manipulative Device: (two players) In turn, take out a cap, read fact, and give answer. Check answer by turning cap over. If correct, keep cap. If incorrect, put it back in the can. The winner is the player with the most caps at the end of the game.

Additional Activities: Use the bottle caps for individual drill.

This activity can be used for addition, subtraction, and division.

In place of bottle caps, use clip clothespins. Write the fact on one side and the answer on the other.

GUMBALL DIVISION

Skill: Division Facts

Purpose: To be able to recall the basic division facts by matching the fact to the answer.

Note: The *quotient* is the answer in division.

MATERIALS: Poster board (9″ × 12″ and 1½″ × 12″), coding label dots, clear self-adhesive paper, grease pencil, construction paper.

CONSTRUCTION OF MANIPULATIVE DEVICE: On the poster board draw and cut out a gumball machine. Make a slide device in the middle of the machine by cutting a slit near the top and bottom of the round part. Make each slit 2″.

Use coding label dots to make a row of gumballs on the right side of the slits. Then fill in the rest of the machine with gumballs.

Use a 1½″ × 12″ piece of poster board to make a strip to fit inside the slits. Divide the strip evenly and in each section place coding label dots of different colors. On each dot write a division fact.

Cover the gumball machine with clear self-adhesive paper. With a grease pencil write the answers for the strip on the row of gumballs to the right of the slide.

Make large gumballs from construction paper to use as the learner's work papers.

DIRECTIONS ON MANIPULATIVE DEVICE: Slide the cardboard strip up and down to match the gumball facts and answers. Write each fact and answer on a paper gumball.

ADDITIONAL ACTIVITIES: Make other strips for other division facts or for multiplication, addition, or subtraction facts.

GOING FISHING

SKILL: Measurement—Inch

PURPOSE: To be able to measure to the nearer inch.

MATERIALS: Yarn, masking tape, coffee can.

CONSTRUCTION OF MANIPULATIVE DEVICE: Cut twenty pieces of yarn to different lengths and attach a piece of masking tape to each to form a tab. Number the tabs 1 to 20. Store pieces of yarn (worms) in a coffee can or other container.

DIRECTIONS ON MANIPULATIVE DEVICE: Take the worms out of the can and measure each one. Number a paper 1 to 20 and write your answers.

ADDITIONAL ACTIVITIES: From construction paper make different fishing object shapes for the learner to measure. (Examples: hook, fishing pole, worm, fish of various lengths.) Make fishing creel pocket from two pieces of construction paper pasted together to store activity pieces.

MEASUREMENT IN THE SAND

SKILL: Measurement—Inch, Half-Inch

PURPOSE: To be able to measure to the nearer inch or half-inch.

MATERIALS: Poster board (24″ × 36″), construction paper, pictures of shells.

CONSTRUCTION OF MANIPULATIVE DEVICE: From construction paper, draw and cut out eight pails and shovels. Glue the pails onto the poster board and leave an opening in the top of each. Number seven of the pails. On the seven pails draw a line to a specific length and on seven shovels, write the lengths of the lines.

Write the directions for the activity on the eighth pail and write the answers on the eighth shovel. Store the shovels in the pail with the directions.

Decorate the rest of the activity with pictures of shells.

DIRECTIONS ON MANIPULATIVE DEVICE: Take the shovels out of the pail. Measure the line on each pail and put the correct shovel into it. Check your answers.

ADDITIONAL ACTIVITIES: Measure the lines on the pails using a centimeter ruler.

Make cutout sand castles of different heights for the learner to measure.

BIBLIOGRAPHY

BASILE, LEONARD J. "Boards You Can Count On," *Early Years* (January 1979), 34–35.

BOGOJAVLENSKY, ANN RAHNASTO et al. *The Great Learning Book.* Menlo Park, California: Addison-Wesley Publishing Company, 1977.

BROSNAHAN, JOANNE PATRICIA, and BARBARA WALTERS MILES. *A Calendar of Home/School Activities.* Santa Monica, California: Goodyear Publishing Company, 1978.

FORTE, IMOGENE, and MARY ANN PANGLE. *Spelling Magic—Activities, Gimmicks, Games Galore for Making Learning Mean Lots More.* Nashville, Tennessee: Incentive Publications, Inc., 1976.

FRANK, MARJORIE. *Kid's Stuff Math—Activities, Games and Ideas for the Elementary Classroom.* Nashville, Tennessee: Incentive Publications, Inc., 1974.

GLAZER, SUSAN MANDEL. *Getting Ready to Read: Creating Readers from Birth to Six.* Englewood Cliffs, New Jersey: Prentice-Hall, Inc., 1980.

GUTZLER, DOROTHY, and HELEN LINN. *110 Reading Comprehension Activities for Primary, Middle and Upper Levels.* Dansville, New York: The Instructor Publications, Inc., 1976.

HIGLEY, JOAN. *Activities Desk Book for Teaching Reading Skills.* West Nyack, New York: Parker Publishing Co., Inc., 1977.

"Hip Pocket Reading Games, Part 2," *Instructor* (May 1979), 5–12.

HURST, CAROL. "Textbooks Plus," *Early Years* (May 1980), 30–56.

HYMAN, RONALD. *Paper, Pencils, and Pennies: Games for Learning and Having Fun.* Englewood Cliffs, New Jersey: Prentice-Hall, Inc., 1977.

KAPLAN, SANDRA NINA et al. *Change for Children.* Santa Monica, California: Goodyear Publishing Company, Inc., 1973.

KEITH, JOY L. *Word Attack Joy.* Naperville, Illinois: Reading Joy, Inc., 1977.

KINDIG, DEAN. *Ready! Set! Game Plans for Winning Readers.* Dansville, New York: The Instructor Publications, Inc., 1978.

LIFSON, ALLAN. *101 Fantastic Funshop Favorites.* Fountain Valley, California: Educational Consultant Group, 1978.

LIU, SARAH, and MARY LOU VITTITOW. *Games Without Losers—Learning Games and Independent Activities for Elementary Classrooms.* Nashville, Tennessee: Incentive Publications, Inc., 1975.

MAGER, ROBERT F. *Preparing Instructional Objectives.* Belmont, California: Fearon Publishers, 1962.

MALLETT, JERRY J. *Classroom Reading Games Activities Kit.* West Nyack, New York: The Center for Applied Research in Education, Inc., 1975.

———. *101 Make and Play Reading Games for the Intermediate Grades.* West Nyack, New York: The Center for Applied Research in Education, Inc., 1976.

MENLOVE, COLEEN, K. *Ready, Set, Go! How to Give Your Children a Head Start Before They Go to School.* Englewood Cliffs, New Jersey: Prentice-Hall, Inc., 1978.

PLATTS, MARY E. *Plus A Handbook of Classroom Ideas to Motivate the Teaching of Elementary Mathematics.* Stevensville, Michigan: Educational Service, Inc., 1975.

———. *Spice: Suggested Activities to Motivate the Teaching of the Language Arts in the Elementary School.* Stevensville, Michigan: Educational Service, Inc., 1973.

RICE, MARY FORMAN, and CHARLES H. FLATTER. *Help Me Learn: A Handbook for Teaching Young Children.* Englewood Cliffs, New Jersey: Prentice-Hall, Inc., 1979.

SALUDIS, ANTHONY J. *Language Arts Activities* (2nd ed.) Dubuque, Iowa: Kendall/Hunt Publishing Company, 1977.

TIEDT, SIDNEY W., and IRIS M. TIEDT. *Elementary Teacher's Complete Ideas Handbook.* Englewood Cliffs, New Jersey: Prentice-Hall, 1970.

THOMPSON, RICHARD A. *Energizers for Reading Instruction.* West Nyack, New York: Parker Publishing Co., Inc., 1973.

WEBER, LOUISE, and M.C. WEBER. *Kids 'N Katalogs.* Nashville, Tennessee: Incentive Publications, Inc., 1975.